Published by Epiphany Publishing
ISBN 979-8-9914788-3-0

To my husband, Ron, for encouraging me to pursue my master's degree when I first learned about communications audits and assessments, and for supporting me as a leadership development coach. To my daughter, whose quick wit keeps me on my toes and humbles me.

Thank you.

I'd also like to thank my longtime friend, journalist Dennis Niemiec, for proofreading my first drafts of this book and offering feedback; my longtime friend and very talented editor, Jennifer Stang of JustWrite, for her final edits and formatting; and my graphic designer, Alex Lumelsky, for his talent and input. Finally, I'm thankful for the feedback I received on the first edition that prompted me to update it and release this second edition.

Table of Contents

"Good communication bridges confusion and clarity."

– Nat Turner

Introduction

I noticed a big communication gap during my third coaching session with a new client. During his first two sessions, Mickey was upbeat and excited about his new position, contrasting it with his last job, which he described as deflating.

He also commended the onboarding process at his new job, which excited me because I had worked with his supervisor on this process. He was the third employee going through the new onboarding program and deemed it "the best onboarding experience" of all his jobs. That was a win.

Mickey entered his third coaching session in a noticeably different mood. His voice was low, and the energy I heard in the last two sessions was no longer there. He seemed a bit angry.

He had just left his 90-day review with his supervisor and human resources, and it didn't go well. He left the meeting with 13 items of what he called "complaints" about him.

We reviewed each item, categorized them as either a critique or an action item, and leaned on his natural talents to develop a game plan. What to do next wasn't the most challenging issue; it was realizing that Mickey and the management had a communication disconnect.

Mickey felt blindsided by the meeting. He told me that the presentation of the list of problems was the first time he had heard of any issue. He was surprised. For 90 days prior, no one had indicated an issue with his performance, he claimed. However, when I later talked to his supervisor, he clarified that he had shared some of Micky's problems with him before the review.

I wondered if management would be surprised to realize the significance of this communication gap, its detrimental impact on the culture, and how it could potentially grow into a more substantial gap if left unaddressed. Communication disconnects can also result in a high turnover of employees.

What this organization needed was a communications assessment or audit. This process would bring such issues to the forefront, allow leadership to address them, and develop a communications strategic plan for implementation in the organization.

How people communicate will ultimately create the work culture. It starts from the top down. Leaders set the tone of any business or organization and impact employee communication, from water cooler chatter to boardroom banter and everything in between.

We must take ownership of our communication by reflecting upon our relationships during times of struggle. Leaders and executives shouldn't fear the results of an assessment. In fact, they should embrace them. It's what they don't know that could negatively affect their bottom line and culture.

Consider your approach to communicating with a significant person in your life. When there is conflict or misunderstanding, do you come with an open mind and heart, seeking to understand and resolve the issue? Or do you come with a loaded question to trap and find fault with the other?

A great number of conflicts in life, including among colleagues, could be resolved if the goal of any conversation was simply to understand the other person, not to trap them or find fault with them.

This is difficult for many people and requires much humility and openness. Commit yourself to seeking open and honest communication; you will find that this commitment brings resolution, peace, and unity. A company's communication should flow freely across all lines and departments, creating an open and honest culture when necessary.

Strengthening the Culture through a Communications Assessment

Conducting a communications assessment, which is like an audit, is a strategic move that can lead to more effective, engaging, and aligned communications practices within an organization. Have you ever been involved in such a process? Don't let the word "audit" scare you. It's truly a tool for assessing communications practices and learning how to improve them to create a productive culture.

When done correctly, a communications audit comprehensively assesses an organization's communications practices, strategies, and channels. It aims to identify strengths and weaknesses and improve communication effectiveness and efficiency. Plus, it involves evaluating how well an organization communicates internally and externally, ensuring alignment with business goals and brand image.

When we conduct an audit, we first decide what we want to assess—internal or external communications. Of course, we can do both. However, we must separate the two and begin with the end in mind, asking questions such as: What are we trying to accomplish? What are we looking to learn?

Ideally, you want to create a creative and engaging culture that drives your organization to prosperity. An audit will reveal disconnects and gaps within communications and show how to close them, connect the dots, and fill in the gaps.

Read on to learn 11 valuable insights leaders gain from assessing communication styles. Drawing on over 25 years of experience in communications, I will explain the value a communications audit brings to a company and how to foster a productive culture within your organization. This new edition is designed as a workbook with exercises and personal reflections on communication styles. After completing the communications audit, leaders discover that the organization can greatly benefit from one-on-one coaching, as well as team-building workshops and group coaching.

I often use the words "audit" and "assessment" interchangeably in this context, but they're not identical. Both are valuable tools, and both can be as surface-level or as in-depth as the situation requires. The key difference lies in how they're perceived and the lens through which they evaluate communication.

An assessment looks at communication through a developmental lens. We can assess an individual, a team, or an entire organization to understand strengths, growth areas, and patterns that influence culture. Assessments tend to feel more approachable because they focus on awareness, learning, and improvement.

An audit, on the other hand, is more comprehensive and systematic. It examines communications practices, processes, and outcomes with a wider scope—almost like a 360-degree view of what's working and what's getting in the way. The word "audit" can sound intimidating because people associate it with money, taxes, or government oversight. But in this context, it's not about catching mistakes or getting anyone "in trouble." It's about clarity, alignment, and strengthening the foundation of how an organization communicates.

Both tools share the same purpose:

- improving communication,
- increasing productivity, and
- ultimately supporting profitability and organizational health

Whether we call it an audit or an assessment, the goal is the same—to help leaders and teams communicate with greater intention, confidence, and impact.

This is an interactive book. You will want to take notes. You can use index cards to write down executive notes, or you can keep a Leadership Communications Journal. Be prepared to answer questions and record observations about your communication styles. Let's get started!

"The single biggest problem in communication is the illusion that it has occurred." – George Bernard Shaw

Insight 1: Communication Channels

We all have our preferred ways of communicating. I'll admit it: I do not enjoy listening to voicemail messages. If you want my attention, send me a short text—not a novel—with just a few clear sentences.

But effective communication isn't about our preferences. It's about understanding how others best receive information. Some people process by talking things through. Others want to read, reflect, and analyze. Our responsibility as communicators is to recognize those differences and adapt.

A perfect example happened within my own family. My sister-in-law and I were both approached—through our husbands—about a potential business opportunity. I insisted on meeting the man behind the proposal. I wanted to look him in the eye, ask questions, and get a feel for who he was. My sister-in-law, on the other hand, had zero interest in meeting him. She preferred to read the business plan and supporting documents.

Here's the funny part: I never read a single document, and she never spoke to the man—yet we both reached the exact same conclusion. The investment was a bad idea. Two completely different communication styles. One shared outcome.

It's a reminder that people absorb information in different ways, and when we honor those differences, we make better decisions and build stronger relationships. Through a communications assessment, leaders can determine which communications channels are most effective and which ones need improvement.

I've worked with some clients where the communication culture was centered on email. This means that most of their communication was written, even when team members were just a few steps away from each other. Some shared the same office, and they still communicated in writing!

Written communication has its benefits. Certain things need to be put into writing, but only in a verbal dialogue can two or more people engage in fruitful conversations that solve problems.

We begin by conducting an inventory of communications touchpoints. Consider every place where your organization interacts with various contacts—whether it's in person or through emails, social media, newsletters, teams, presentations, texts, or other channels.

Remember, everything associated with your brand counts. How is your staff communicating internally? This same inventory can be used for external communications.

Nonverbal communication contributes more than 50% of how we communicate. Albert Mehrabian, a body language researcher, broke down the components of a face-to-face conversation. He found that communication is 55% nonverbal, 38% vocal, and 7% words only.

Essentially, when we engage in written communication, we lose more than 50 percent of how we communicate, including facial expressions, tone of voice, and body language. In some cases, sarcasm is lost. People might perceive a written message differently than if they were with you face-to-face.

In one client case, an executive team member noted that email communication was often a method to pass off responsibility. It was common in their company's culture for employees to send an email expressing concern or an issue and copy dozens of people, as if passing the buck to someone else.

"Sending the email meant to them, they are taking it off their plate, and someone else needs to figure this out," the executive said. "They often don't single out any one person, so no one knows who that person is addressing … what happens is no one takes ownership of the issue, and that person who sent the email says, 'Well, I told you guys.'"

In a communications audit, we can gain insights regarding data, numbers, percentages, and written statements. In one client audit, it was determined that more than 50% of employees communicate through email. There were also disagreements on the effectiveness of email versus face-to-face conversations.

Some employees preferred face-to-face meetings with follow-up emails confirming what was discussed. Others thought emails delayed problem-solving, and impromptu face-to-face meetings were distracting.

This is an important starting point. Leadership needs to understand how employees communicate within the workplace. As other employees noted, emails have value because they create a paper trail for coworkers who claim amnesia or are so disorganized that they do not keep track of communication. They document what was discussed and remind people what needs to be done.

Know what platforms your team members are using regularly. The effectiveness of those platforms needs to be assessed, as well. Think about what else can be learned about the communications channels.

Step into the Channels

"The most important thing in communication is hearing what isn't said."
– Peter F. Drucker

Evaluate What's Happening

- **Audit Touchpoints:** Map out all internal and external communications channels: email, chat, meetings, intranet, newsletters, social media, etc.—and assess frequency, audience, and purpose.
- **Review Analytics:** Use platform metrics (like open rates, read receipts, and engagement stats) to understand what's landing and what's getting lost.
- **Shadow Communications:** Sit in on meetings, listen to team calls, or ask for access to typical messaging threads to observe tone, clarity, and effectiveness firsthand.

Gain Insights from People—Not Just Platforms

- **Ask Targeted Questions:** In town halls or in one-on-one sessions, pose reflective prompts, like:
  o What feels clear and helpful in how we communicate?
  o Where do you feel disconnected or confused?

- **Tap into Subcultures:** Different departments may have entirely different norms. Connect with informal leaders to hear the "unofficial" narrative around communications.

Close the Loop

- **Build Feedback Rhythms:** Encourage ongoing feedback via surveys, suggestion boxes, or quarterly retrospectives. Use prompts like: What would make our communications more engaging or empowering?
- **Celebrate What Works:** When a channel improves engagement or clarity, spotlight it across the organization to model success.

Reflect and Reframe

- **Story Map Your Messaging:** Do your communications reinforce the mission and values? Try visually mapping how each channel contributes to that story.
- **Use Metaphor or Infused Reflection:** Invite teams to consider their role as "light bearers" or "bridge builders" in how they share truth and cultivate connection.

Leadership Communications Reflection Card

Create your reflective cards or journal to evaluate patterns, success, and areas for improvement. Take note of what you are noticing.

Theme: Shaping Culture Through Clarity and Connection

1. Where Am I Heard?

Consider:

- Which channels consistently yield engagement or feedback?
- Where do my words spark action, not confusion?

Prompt:

Think of a moment when your message deeply resonated with a team or individual. What made that communication meaningful? What channel did you use?

2. Where Does Clarity Break Down?

Consider:

- Which modes of communication feel inconsistent or misaligned with intent?
- Are there gaps between what I mean and what others receive?

Prompt:

Reflect on a time when a message didn't land well. Was it the platform, the tone, the timing—or something deeper?

3. Am I Modeling Communication Worth Repeating?

Consider:

- How does my style create ripple effects in organizational culture?
- Do I affirm, empower, and connect—or unintentionally complicate?

Prompt:

Imagine your style being replicated by future and emerging leaders in the organization. What aspects would uplift your team's culture? What parts might need adjusting?

4. How Does My Voice Reflect My Values and Calling?

Value-Infused Reframe:

Communication is stewardship—a chance to reflect the light of truth, compassion, and purpose. Let your conversation reflect your values.

Prompt:

Think about the role your voice plays within your organization. What message has been entrusted to you to carry, and through which channels might it be best delivered?

"When people talk, listen completely. Most people never listen." – Ernest Hemingway

Insight 2: Communicate Consistency

It never ceases to amaze me—and many of my colleagues in the communications field—how often organizations dedicated to messaging and outreach fail to communicate consistently with their own internal teams. These are professionals who spend their days crafting compelling narratives, shaping public perception, and delivering polished messages to the outside world. Yet inside their own walls, employees are left guessing, piecing together information, or feeling completely out of the loop.

It's one of the great ironies of our profession: Organizations that excel at external communication often struggle the most with internal communication.

One of the first questions I ask leaders during coaching sessions is, "How often do you go on a listening tour?" I used to ask this of every client running for public office. Any true public servant must understand what's on the minds of their constituents. The same principle applies to leadership in any organization—you must listen more than you speak. The old saying resonates so deeply: God gave us two ears and one mouth for a reason.

A communications assessment helps leaders understand how well they are maintaining brand communication with all stakeholders—employees, clients, partners, and the broader community. It clarifies how your organization interacts with the world by examining whether your messaging aligns with your brand image, values, and business goals.

Ask yourself: Are your messages consistent across audiences, channels, and contexts?

A communications audit reveals whether your organization presents a unified brand impression or sends mixed signals that confuse people inside and outside the organization.

And here's another essential question: What is your story, and how are you telling it?

Every organization has a story—a purpose, a mission, a reason for existing. To build a recognizable brand identity, that story must be told repeatedly, consistently, and creatively across multiple platforms. Repetition isn't redundancy; it's reinforcement.

This becomes even more critical during a crisis. Consistency, accuracy, and a single unified voice are non-negotiable. When I consult on crisis communications, the first step is identifying one spokesperson and crafting one clear message. The "one person, one message" protocol minimizes misinformation, prevents contradictory statements, and maintains credibility when it matters most.

I was brought in to consult with an organization that found itself in the middle of a crisis. They initially tried to manage the situation internally, and when that didn't work, they sought advice from a veteran public relations specialist—but only on a pro-bono, informal basis. The issue involved a public-private partnership with the city of Detroit, which added another layer of complexity and scrutiny.

When I was asked to step in, the first thing I did was identify a single spokesperson. At the time, two different individuals were speaking to the media, and each was giving a different version of events. The result was predictable: confusion, distrust, and the appearance that the organization had something to hide.

I recommended appointing a different spokesperson—someone articulate, polished, and well-versed on the issue. From that point forward, he became the sole voice addressing the crisis. Shortly after establishing one clear, consistent messenger, the situation stabilized, the narrative became coherent, and the crisis was ultimately defused.

Consistency also applies to timing and delivery. Some organizations send a weekly newsletter at the same time every week—and their employees come to rely on it. When my daughter was in high school, I often wished her school would adopt the same practice. Parents would have been far less stressed if we knew exactly when to expect important updates.

The same principle applies to social media. In workshops I've attended, LinkedIn strategists recommend responding to at least three posts three days a week—and posting your own content at least three days a week. Consistency fuels the algorithm, but more importantly, it keeps you top-of-mind with the people you want to reach.

In 2025, I committed to sharing regular "Epiphany Insights"—short reflections on leadership, communication, and personal growth. It mirrors the weekly rhythm of my blog. We learn something new every day, so why not share those lessons with others?

A communications audit or assessment provides a roadmap for crafting clear, consistent messaging that resonates with employees. Internal understanding of the brand is just as important as external perception. If your own people don't know the organization's mission, vision, and goals, how can they possibly communicate them to clients or customers?

Supervisors also play a critical role. During sessions, I often ask employees: How often does your direct supervisor keep you informed about company directives, issues, and challenges? The answers are revealing—and they often highlight gaps leaders didn't know existed.

Your organization is only as strong as the communication within it. Inconsistency breeds confusion. I've coached many clients who arrive frustrated because they weren't informed about something that directly affected their work. When employees are left in the dark, they can't perform at their best.

You want your people focused on their responsibilities—not distracted by communication breakdowns. Frustration drains energy, creativity, and productivity. This is why I encourage leaders to schedule regular Listening Tours. Spend time in different departments. Sit with team leaders, supervisors, and managers. Ask questions. Observe. Listen. These conversations help you understand what's working, what's not, and what your people need to thrive. They allow you to meet individuals where they are on their work journey.

Listen and learn.

Then, ask yourself: What new insights can consistent communication reveal—and how will you use them to strengthen your culture?

"Pay less attention to what men say. Just watch what they do." – Dale Carnegie

1. Assess for Alignment

- **Mission Check:** Compare messaging across channels (emails, newsletters, meetings, onboarding materials) with core values and purpose. Are tone and emphasis consistent?
- **Department Voice Scan:** Evaluate whether different departments share similar messaging around priorities, metrics, and expectations—or if silos are creating contradictory signals.

2. Check for Cognitive Dissonance

- **Words vs. Behavior:** Assess whether leadership communications align with observable behaviors. Inconsistencies between "what we say" and "what we do" erode trust.
- **Systemic Signals:** Review processes, policies, and recognition systems. Do they reinforce the same values that your communications highlight?

3. Use People as Mirrors

- **360 reviews**—also known as 360-degree feedback—are a comprehensive performance evaluation method where feedback is gathered from multiple sources surrounding an employee. Instead of relying solely on a manager's perspective, this approach includes input from:

- Supervisors
- Peers
- Direct reports
- Self-assessment
- (Sometimes) clients or external stakeholders

- **The Power of 360 Feedback:** Ask key team members at different levels to describe your vision or values in their own words. Notice patterns—or the lack of them.
    - 360 reviews are especially powerful in leadership development, team-building initiatives, and coaching contexts. They're not meant to replace performance reviews but to complement them with richer, more nuanced feedback. They should include:
        - **Self-evaluation**, where the employee also completes a self-assessment to compare perceptions;
        - **Anonymous responses**, because feedback is collected anonymously to encourage honesty; and
        - **Rating and comments**, because participants typically use a rating scale and provide written comments on competencies like communication, leadership, collaboration, and reliability.

- **Notice Gossip Loops:** Listen to informal channels. Is gossip consistently happening in the workplace? What's being said in the margins? Inconsistencies often show up in hallway conversations before they're formally identified.

4. Establish Feedback Rhythms

- **Pulse Surveys:** Use simple, recurring questions, like:
  - What did you hear in that message?
  - What do you still need clarified?
  - What information was helpful?
- **Listening Labs:** Create safe spaces for teams to explore how communications impact clarity, decision-making, and morale.

5. Visualize the Messaging Ecosystem

- **Mapping Tool:** Chart major communication flows and their senders, frequency, and purpose. Look for overlaps, contradictions, or gaps.
- **Narrative Tracking:** Reflect on how the organization's story evolves across different messages. Is the thread strong and coherent—or fraying?

6. Stewardship of Voice

- **Offer Personal Reflection:** This can deepen the leadership lens. Consistency isn't just strategic—it's a discipline. Executives are stewards of truth and culture; their words must be rooted in integrity, clarity, and grace. Let your "yes" be "yes" and your "no" be "no."

Leadership Diagnostic Card

Theme: Consistency as Culture Crafting

Every message we send either builds coherence or invites confusion. Let's reflect on the signals you're sending— intentionally or not.

1. Where Am I Consistently Understood?

Consider:

- Which messages are repeated back to me with clarity?
- What values or priorities do I have across teams?

Prompt:

Identify one to two phrases or ideas that teammates often quote or reference. How do those messages mirror your intended vision?

2. Where Might Mixed Messages Live?

Consider:

- Are there places where my tone shifts?
- Do my emails say "collaboration," but my Key Performance Indicators (KPIs) reward competition?

Prompt:

Describe a recent moment when messaging or behavior felt inconsistent. What impact did that misalignment have?

3. Am I Mirroring Clarity at Every Level?

Consider:

- Does my team see consistent signals in meetings, metrics, and memos?
- What's modeled from my executive circle outward?

Prompt:

If your frontline team were asked to describe leadership priorities, what would they say? Would it match your vision statement?

4. Integrity in Leadership Voice

Mean what you say. Don't be ambiguous.

Prompt:

Reflect: Where am I called to align my voice more deeply with my calling? What truth needs greater consistency in how I lead, speak, and decide?

Emerging Leader Reflection Card

Theme: Cultivating Consistency with Influence and Intent

You may not craft every message—but your presence shapes how they're received.

1. What Am I Known For?

Consider:

- What words, values, or attitudes do others associate with me?
- Does my presence reinforce or disrupt team alignment?

Prompt:

Write down three things your teammates would likely say about how you communicate or show up. Which of those reflects your true intent?

2. Where Do My Words and Actions Drift Apart?

Consider:

- Do I say, "Let's collaborate," but avoid tough conversations?
- Is my silence sometimes interpreted as agreement or dismissal?

Prompt:

Reflect on a recent moment when your messaging didn't match your behavior—or when someone misunderstood you. What shift could bring more clarity next time?

3. How Am I Holding the Thread of Culture?

Consider:

- Even informal leaders reinforce consistency through tone, storytelling, and behavior.
- Your contribution matters—even when you're not holding a mic.

Prompt:

What's one small way you can reinforce clarity and consistency in your team this week—through how you communicate, encourage, or model?

4. Influence with Stewardship

Your voice—spoken or silent—is part of the calling to lead with integrity.

Prompt:

Discern: What kind of example are you being called to offer in this season—especially through how you communicate truth and compassion?

"To effectively communicate, we must realize that we are all different in the way we perceive the world and use this understanding as a guide to our communication with others." – Tony Robbins

Insight 3: Resources

Why Tools, Training, and Systems Shape the Culture You Create

A few months into a new job, I asked a relative how things were going. He paused, then said something I hear far too often: "It's okay, but I feel like I'm left to figure things out on my own. The training is virtually nonexistent, and it's frustrating."

His experience is not an outlier. Many employees walk into new roles excited to contribute, only to discover that the resources they need—training, documentation, and clarity—are missing. They're expected to perform without the tools required to succeed. And when that happens, frustration becomes the culture.

The Hidden Cost of Missing Resources

In my consulting practice, I often recommend a structured 90-day onboarding process that includes shadowing, daily instruction, and written materials outlining responsibilities and workflows. When organizations invest in this level of preparation, employees feel supported, confident, and aligned. But when they don't, the consequences ripple.

A few years ago, I coached several employees at the same company. Their biggest frustration wasn't the workload or the expectations—it was the absence of resources. Manuals didn't exist. Instructions for operating machinery or completing routine processes were nowhere to be found. Managers were creating documents on the fly, often after mistakes had already occurred.

The result was predictable:

- High turnover
- Low morale
- Repeated errors
- Employees who felt defeated before they even began

These employees weren't resistant to learning. They were starved of the tools that would allow them to do their jobs well. When resources are missing, people don't just struggle—they disengage.

A Communications Assessment: Your Organizational Health Check

A communications assessment functions like a health check for your organization's messaging. It reveals:

- What information is landing
- What's being ignored
- Where confusion is slowing down productivity
- Which channels are effective and which are simply noise

By analyzing how information flows through your organization, you can reallocate resources with intention—investing more in what works and eliminating what doesn't.

This process often uncovers surprising insights:

- Employees may read the weekly email but ignore the intranet
- Teams may rely heavily on text messages rather than formal updates
- Virtual meetings may be overused, underused, or misused
- Some departments may be drowning in information, while others receive almost none

When leaders understand how employees consume information, they can tailor resources to support clarity, consistency, and connection.

Building a Resource-Rich Communication Environment

To communicate effectively and efficiently, organizations must assess the tools they already have—and identify the ones they still need. Consider implementing or strengthening:

1. Employee Communication Platforms
- Tools such as internal communication apps, intranet systems, and instant messaging platforms help streamline updates and keep teams aligned. Commonly used platforms include Monday.com, Slack, and Deel—listed here only as examples, not endorsements.

2. Centralized Resource Libraries
A digital hub where employees can access:
- Manuals
- Policies
- Training materials
- Safety guidelines
- Compliance updates

This reduces confusion and minimizes repetitive questions.

3. Simple, Consistent Messaging Tools

- Sometimes, simplicity is the most powerful approach. A well-written company or HR newsletter can keep employees informed about updates, policies, events, and organizational news. When done consistently, it helps employees feel connected to the mission and to one another.

4. A Dedicated HR Webpage

A password-protected section of your website can house:

- FAQs
- Handbook updates
- Holiday schedules
- Vacation and leave policies
- Safety and compliance information

This becomes a one-stop hub for clarity.

Creating Space for Dialogue

Resources aren't just documents or platforms—they're also opportunities for connection. Consider implementing a "Human Resources Open House" through regular video chats or virtual office hours. This creates a predictable space where employees can:

- Ask questions
- Share concerns
- Receive updates
- Build trust with leadership

It signals transparency, accessibility, and a genuine commitment to employee well-being.

The Leadership Lens: Resources Reflect Your Values

When leaders provide clear, accessible, and consistent resources, they communicate something powerful: *"We want you to succeed, and we're committed to supporting you."*

But when resources are missing, the message becomes equally clear—though far less intentional: *"You're on your own."*

Employees feel the difference immediately. Resources are not just tools; they are cultural signals. They shape how people feel, how they perform, and how long they stay.

Every organization communicates a message through its resources—or its lack of them. When you invest in tools, training, and systems, you're not just improving efficiency. You're building trust. You're creating clarity. You're empowering people to bring their best to the work.

Resources are not an expense. They are an expression of leadership.

Case Study: When Missing Resources Become a Cultural Roadblock
Company: Lakeside Manufacturing (Fictional)
Industry: Industrial equipment
Size: 250 employees

This is a fictional example based on various clients and research on understanding communication dynamics. "Lakeside Manufacturing" faced a familiar but costly problem: high turnover among new hires. Employees were leaving within the first six months, and exit interviews revealed a consistent theme—confusion, frustration, and a lack of training.

The Challenge

New employees were expected to operate complex machinery, follow strict safety protocols, and meet production quotas. Yet the company had:
- No onboarding manual
- No written instructions for machinery
- No standardized training schedule
- No central place to access policies or procedures
- Managers creating documents reactively, often after mistakes occurred

Supervisors were overwhelmed, employees were anxious, and the organization was losing both time and money. One employee summed it up during a coaching session: "I want to do well here, but I feel like I'm guessing every day."

The Turning Point

When leadership agrees to undergo a full communications assessment. The findings are often eye-opening:
- Employees relied heavily on verbal instructions, which varied from manager to manager
- Important updates were buried in long email chains
- Safety protocols were inconsistently communicated
- New hires had no clear roadmap for their first 90 days
- Managers were spending hours each week answering the same questions

The assessment made one thing clear: The issue wasn't employee performance. It was the absence of resources.

The Solution

The suggestion is to implement a structured, resource-rich communication system that includes:

1. A 90-Day Onboarding Plan
- Week-by-week expectations
- Shadowing schedules
- Daily check-ins
- Clear learning milestones

2. A Centralized Resource Library
A password-protected intranet page housing:
- Machinery manuals
- Safety procedures
- HR policies
- Step-by-step workflow guides
- Video demonstrations

3. A Weekly Operations Newsletter
Short, consistent updates that replaced scattered emails and reduced confusion.

4. Manager Toolkits
Templates for:
- Performance conversations
- Training checklists
- Shift handoff notes
- Safety reminders

5. Monthly "Ask HR Anything" Virtual Office Hours
A space for employees to ask questions, clarify policies, and build trust with leadership.

The Results

This is the goal:
- Turnover is reduced
- Training time decreased by a significant percentage because materials were standardized
- Safety incidents declined due to consistent communication
- Managers gained back hours each week previously spent answering repetitive questions
- Employee satisfaction scores increased, especially among new hires

One supervisor said at a company that the goal is, "For everyone to be on the same page. We don't want to reinvent the wheel every day."

The Lesson

A story like this illustrates a powerful truth: Resources are not optional—they are foundational. When employees have access to clear, consistent, and accessible tools, they don't just perform better. They feel valued, supported, and connected to the organization's mission. Resources shape culture, and culture shapes results.

"It doesn't matter how many resources you have. If you don't know how to use them, it will never be enough."
– Unknown

Gaining Insight into Company Resources to Strengthen Communication and Culture

1. Inventory: What's Already Available?

- **Internal Tools:** Review platforms like the intranet, newsletters, dashboards, training portals, and onboarding packets—what tone and message do they convey? Review manuals, HR materials, note-taking, and manager instructions. Note what is resonating and where the gaps exist.
- **Human Assets:** Recognize culture carriers—mentors, team leaders, informal influencers—who shape communication norms and values daily.
- **Previous Initiatives:** Audit past campaigns, workshops, or retreats. What messaging stuck? What faded?

Prompt:

What resources are silently shaping culture behind the scenes? Where might small tweaks yield outsized clarity or engagement?

2. Uncover Hidden Gaps or Overlaps

- **Channel Mapping:** Identify overlapping platforms (e.g., multiple newsletters, outdated manuals, outdated HR resources, or redundant updates). Streamlining boosts clarity.
- **Role Clarity:** Are communication responsibilities well defined? Who owns what message?
- **Support Systems:** Check if teams have access to facilitation guides, value statements, or onboarding scripts—or if they're reinventing the wheel.

Prompt:

Are your resources intuitive, accessible, and consistent—or are teams navigating a maze?

3. Invite Collaborative Insight

- **Culture Champions Circles:** Bring together informal influencers to discuss what communications resources feel empowering—and what feels outdated.
- **Peer Coaching:** Encourage emerging leaders to reflect on resource use: What tools helped them feel connected and were clear when they first joined?

Prompt:

What resources feel like a bridge? What feels like a barrier?

4. Co-Design for Impact and Identity

- **Customize Templates and Toolkits:** Involve diverse teams in shaping guides, scripts, or visuals that reflect your culture and mission.
- **Visual and Storytelling Layer:** Use metaphors (like "threads," "lighthouses," or "ripples") to bring abstract values to life.

Prompt:

Which resource could benefit from a refresh—not just in design, but in spirit?

5. Stewardship of the Message

Resources aren't just tools; they're entrusted gifts. Use them to serve with truth, connection, and grace.

Prompt:

What message have you been entrusted to carry? How might your current resources reflect—or distort—that calling?

Leadership Reflection Card

Theme: Resource Stewardship for Cultural Clarity

Resources aren't just tools—they're signals. What we choose to invest in speaks volumes.

1. What Resources Are Quietly Shaping Our Culture?

Consider:

- What templates, onboarding materials, or messaging flows are used regularly?
- Are they reinforcing the values you intend?

Prompt:

Identify one internal tool or guide your team often uses. Does it reflect your vision—or need a refresh?

2. Where Are We Reinventing Instead of Refining?

Consider:

- Do teams create their own communications or culture-building materials from scratch?
- Are existing resources accessible, intuitive, and aligned?

Prompt:

Describe a time when a lack of resource clarity caused confusion or duplication. What system or guide could have helped?

3. Who Holds the Unspoken Influence?

Consider:

- Which team members model clarity, consistency, and connection—without being asked?
- How might you better equip or celebrate them?

Prompt:

Name someone whose presence quietly strengthens communication and culture. What resource could amplify their impact?

4. Stewardship Framing: Stewardship over Stockpile

Resources are gifts entrusted for truth-minded leadership. They're meant to uplift, empower, and clarify—not clutter or confuse.

Prompt:

Reflect: What resource in your organization needs your heart—not just your signature? How might your stewardship of communication tools reflect true alignment?

Culture Champion Reflection Card

Theme: Everyday Stewardship of Resources and Culture

You don't need a title to shape the atmosphere—just intention, care, and clarity.

1. Which Tools Do I Use Most Often?

Consider:

- What platforms, guides, or templates do I rely on?
- Do they reinforce connection and clarity—or need adaptation?

Prompt:

List two to three resources you use to share updates, train teammates, or express values. What message do those tools subtly carry?

2. Where Could I Improve Consistency or Clarity?

Consider:

- Do I have access to visual guides, core messaging, or onboarding support?
- Do teammates receive conflicting information, depending on where they look?

Prompt:

Recall a time when mixed messages or unclear tools created tension. What small shift would have created more alignment?

3. How Do I Help Others Feel Connected?

Consider:

- Which part of my role supports team morale or shared understanding?
- Am I helping others navigate the unspoken norms?

Prompt:

Think of someone you recently helped feel "at home" in your organization. What resource, attitude, or example helped the most?

4. Culture as Calling

Creating clarity and alignment isn't just practical—it's compassionate leadership. You're bearing invisible weight on behalf of others.

Prompt:

Reflect in journaling: *Where am I called to be a cultural gardener—tending clarity, kindness, and connection with what's in my hands? Which resource could I nurture or refresh to serve others better?*

"I began noting where the audience laughed or clapped or paid the closest attention. I came to realize that a good speech is not a soliloquy but a dialogue."
– Sarah Ferguson, The Duchess of York

Insight 4: Employee Engagement and Feedback

When I talk about leadership, I always return to the "AB and the Three Cs": Always Be Connecting, Community, and Collaborating with the Community. Why? Because at the heart of every thriving business, every meaningful relationship, and every strong neighborhood is one essential ingredient—connection.

I witnessed that truth in action at the 2025 Western Wayne Business Leadership Banquet in Southeast Michigan. It wasn't just another networking event. It was a masterclass in humility, purpose, and the power of building something larger than ourselves. The banquet has become one of the premier networking gatherings in the region, led with excellence by the Livonia-Westland Chamber of Commerce.

Dan West, the chamber's president and CEO, is one of the most engaging leaders I've had the privilege to work with. We met early in our journalism careers, long before either of us imagined where our paths would lead. Our careers took turns we didn't expect, yet those early newsroom experiences became the foundation for the leadership styles we eventually developed—rooted in curiosity, communication, and connection.

One voice that truly stood out was the keynote speaker, who, when asked about her leadership style, said: "I enjoy being part of a team … I'd much rather be part of a championship team than be the champion. I think it's so much more rewarding to do it together," said Linda Hubbard, CEO of Carhartt.

That quote stuck with me. Real leadership isn't about spotlighting yourself—it's about lifting up others and creating something enduring, together.

Let's keep connecting. Let's keep building. Let's lead with purpose. You do that by being engaged. That doesn't mean just walking around asking people how they are doing. It means really getting to know people and their strengths, weaknesses, and what motivates them.

A communications assessment reveals how well employees are receiving and understanding information. When I facilitated a focus group for an emerging association of women business owners and professionals, I asked each participant to introduce herself using what I call the "Four Cs."

I instructed them to share who they are and what they do by describing the Cartoon Character, Car, Color, and Cuisine that best represent them. The exercise immediately sparked engagement. People laughed, opened up, and connected in ways that traditional introductions rarely inspire.

This same activity works beautifully in organizational team-building sessions. You don't have to become best friends with your coworkers, but research consistently shows that vulnerability builds trust. And trust is the foundation of effective collaboration. Getting to know colleagues on a more personal level isn't frivolous—it's strategic.

When I served as press secretary for Wayne County in Michigan, I helped launch an internal newsletter designed to help employees learn more about one another. One of my first interviews was with a Homeland Security employee who stood more than 6 feet 5 inches and looked like a lumberjack.

To my surprise, he loved to knit. Hats, scarves—he made them all. His hobby didn't match the tough exterior people saw at work, but employees loved discovering this unexpected side of him. It humanized him and reminded everyone that people are always more layered than their job titles.

In coaching sessions, I often encourage managers to create similar opportunities for conversation. When coworkers understand one another's personalities, interests, and strengths, they build trust—and trust fuels productivity.

Evaluating your internal communication methods also helps you assess employee engagement and whether you're truly fostering it. Effective internal communication aligns with business goals, enhances engagement, and promotes transparency and collaboration. Team-building exercises, off-site meetings, and workshops can all support this effort.

At one organization I worked with, a staff member shared how the new vice president invited the team to a casual meeting over pizza and asked everyone to share an interesting fact about themselves. It was the first time management had ever shown interest in employees' lives.

Staff members later said it was the best company meeting they'd ever attended. One remarked, "Usually, the president or VP pontificates for 45 minutes and then goes back to his office, never engaging any of us in a dialogue." A simple gesture made employees feel seen and valued.

Leadership that lasts begins with engagement that sticks. As a coach guiding emerging leaders and executives, I see a recurring truth: Employee engagement isn't a feel-good HR buzzword—it's a strategic advantage. When done well, it reduces turnover, strengthens trust, and builds cultures people want to stay in.

Dale Carnegie's research reinforces this. Two-thirds of leaders who practice daily employee engagement report lower-than-average turnover. When engagement becomes infrequent, that benefit drops sharply. The message is clear: Engagement must be consistent and intentional.

Engagement also requires understanding your own strengths and weaknesses—and those of your team. That's why I became a certified CliftonStrengths® Coach and why I facilitate strengths-based team-building workshops.

The CliftonStrengths assessment, formerly StrengthsFinder, is a widely used Gallup tool that identifies your natural talents in thinking, feeling, and behaving. It categorizes these talents into 34 themes and helps you develop them into strengths that fuel personal and professional growth. By focusing on what you do best, you increase engagement, productivity, and overall well-being. The assessment presents paired statements for you to choose from, revealing your top themes—such as Futuristic, Achiever, or Empathy—and offering insights on how to leverage them.

Gallup research indicates that people who focus on using their strengths are three times more likely to report having an excellent quality of life and six times more likely to be engaged in their jobs.

Creating a strengths-based culture means knowing the strengths of each team member and intentionally using them. Incorporating this assessment into your communications plan can significantly improve employee engagement.

Ten people can look at the same challenge and come up with 10 different solutions because each person brings unique experiences, strengths, and even weaknesses to the table.

In my workshops, I help employees recognize their own strengths as well as the strengths and growth areas of their colleagues. When leaders tap into this awareness, they're able to build stronger teams and create work cultures where people—and performance—truly thrive.

Our strengths and weaknesses shape how we show up at work and how we relate to the people around us. They influence the way we communicate, collaborate, and solve problems. They're also foundational in developing leadership styles and advancing in our careers. Understanding your natural talents is the starting point of self-awareness—and the heart of my coaching approach.

"Create caring and robust connections between every employee and their work, customers, leaders, managers, and the organization to achieve results that matter to everyone in this sentence." – David Zinger

What Does Intentional Engagement Look Like?

Let's break it down with four goal-setting strategies that anchor meaningful employee experiences:

1. **Recruitment Goals:** Don't just hire for the job—hire for *culture*. The most successful teams begin by finding candidates who match the values, rhythm, and spirit of your organization. Retention starts at hello.
2. **Hiring Goals:** A 2018 Jobvite survey revealed that **33% of employees quit within the first 90 days**. What's the fix? Smooth onboarding, clear expectations, and a sense of belonging from day one. First impressions are lasting ones.
3. **Job Satisfaction Goals:** Engagement grows when employees do work, they find their work *important and interesting*. Leaders ask: Is this person in a role that fuels their strengths? People thrive when their talents are aligned with their tasks.
4. **Disengagement Goals:** Surprisingly, intentional disengagement is also key. Breaks, mental health support, and boundaries are vital. Encouraging restorative time off empowers better focus and productivity when it's time to re-engage.

Engagement isn't a strategy—it's a relationship. Too often, retention is approached as a checklist or a policy. However, genuine loyalty stems from relationships founded on clarity, connection, and care. Daily engagement is the human side of leadership—and it's non-negotiable for teams that want to thrive.

Whether you're hiring your first team member or leading a national workforce, start with presence. The kind that notices, listens, and affirms. The kind that dares to ask: Does this person feel seen? That's where transformation begins.

Leaders can learn to coach in a way that fosters connection.

Leader Reflection Card

1. Prioritize Purpose and Strengths

- Align roles with individual talents and values.

- Use tools like CliftonStrengths, DISC, Myers-Briggs, and, of course, the Epiphany Communications Assessment to help employees see how their contributions matter.

Prompt:

Outline the talents of each team member. Ask: How can partner team members be based on strengths?

2. Create Feedback Loops, Not Bottlenecks

- Encourage two-way feedback; leaders should ask for input as often as they give it.

- Use pulse surveys or open-ended prompts like, "What's one thing that would help you thrive this week?"

Prompt:

Journal what patterns are surfacing. What are you noticing about yourself?

3. Recognize and Reward Often

- Celebrate small wins publicly.

- Use specific praise tied to impact: "Your clarity in yesterday's meeting helped the team move forward."

4. Balance Workloads to Prevent Burnout

- Regularly audit team capacity.

- Ask: "What's draining your energy right now?" and "Where do you feel most alive in your work?"

5. Invest in Growth

- Offer mentorship, stretch assignments (which prompt staff members to work on projects outside their comfort zones), learning stipends, and, of course, coaching.

- Frame development as a shared journey, not a performance fix.

Exercises to Spark Insight and Engagement

Here are a few creative, low-lift activities that can be used in team meetings, retreats, or coaching sessions:

Glow and Grow

- Each person shares one recent success ("Glow") and one area for improvement ("Grow").
- Peers offer affirming feedback and suggestions for growth.
  - Benefit: Great for building psychological safety and self-awareness.

Feedback Circles

- Small groups share one accomplishment and one challenge.
- Others offer constructive feedback and encouragement.
  - Benefit: Promotes empathy and shared learning.

Anonymous Feedback Box

- Leave a physical or digital box open for ongoing feedback.
- Review themes regularly and respond transparently.
  - Benefit: Builds trust and surfaces hidden concerns.

Feedback Through Art

- Invite team members to draw or visually represent how they feel about their work or team dynamics.

- Use metaphors like bridges, ripples, or compasses to guide reflection.

  - Benefit: Ideal for creative teams or faith-based settings.

Reflection Card: The Engagement Compass

Theme: Navigating What Matters Most

Visual Metaphor: A compass with four quadrants—North (Purpose), East (Energy), South (Support), West (Voice)

The Compass Image:

You can visualize or sketch a simple compass with these labels:

- **North – Purpose**
- **East – Energy**
- **South – Support**
- **West – Voice**

Each direction represents a key dimension of engagement.

Reflection Prompts:

Invite leaders or team members to reflect on each quadrant:

North – Purpose

- What part of your work feels most meaningful right now?
- Where do you see your strengths making a difference?

East – Energy

- What's fueling your energy this week?
- What's draining it—and how can we shift that?

South – Support

- Who's showing up for you—and how?
- What kind of support would help you thrive?

West – Voice

- When was the last time you felt truly heard?
- What feedback or idea do you wish you could share?

"You never know when a moment and a few sincere words can have an impact on a life." – Zig Ziglar

Insight 5: Crafting Clear Messaging and Compelling Content

Strong communication is the backbone of organizational success. Messaging and content creation work hand-in-hand to inspire alignment, build trust, and define a company's brand. Clear, consistent messaging resonates with employees and external stakeholders alike. It inspires confidence and drives appropriate action across the organization.

Messaging: Speaking with One Voice

In times of crisis, consistency is critical—if you are scrambling to craft messaging after the fact, you are already behind. One employee I interviewed during a communications audit expressed frustration: "What I find most frustrating is being given a directive by one supervisor and then another directive by another supervisor, and that second directive conflicts with the first directive. Management never seems to be on the same page."

This disconnect underscores the importance of unified messaging. Every employee should know the company's vision, mission, and goals. That knowledge forms the foundation of a strong culture and positions the organization for success. Messaging also defines the brand.

When I begin working with a client, I ask standard questions to gauge alignment:

1. What is it you get paid to do?
2. What is the company's vision?
3. What are the current quarterly goals?
4. What are some of the current challenges?

These questions reveal whether employees understand their environment and whether the company is speaking in one voice. Leaders must also ask themselves: How well do I understand what employees know about our company, and how they are communicating our narrative?

Messaging is not just what you say—it's how you say it. It ties directly to the platforms you use, the consistency of your communications, and even nonverbal cues. As my father, Sabri Mansour Denha, often reminded me, "No one cares what you have to say if you don't know how to say it."

Effective messaging requires:

- Knowing your audience and shaping words to fit their knowledge, culture, and expectations.
- Brevity and directness, using strong, simple language that avoids jargon.
- Introducing the most important point immediately.
- Organizing ideas logically, reinforced with visuals or clear calls to action.

Avoid pitfalls such as overwhelming people with detail, relying on technical terms that alienate, overlooking cultural differences, or failing to provide a clear next step. To craft strong messages, define your purpose, identify your audience, distill your core idea into one sentence, refine for clarity, test it outside the context, and present it with structure and supporting visuals.

Content: Telling Your Story

If messaging is the leader's voice, content is the organization's voice. Content creation ensures the company's narrative reaches employees, customers, and the broader community.

When I served as press secretary for the Wayne County Executive, I wrote his talking points and responded to media questions on his behalf. It took years to fully understand his communication style, priorities, and the county's initiatives so I could create content that reflected his voice and advanced our goals. I also wrote content for other departments within the county, and there were more than 10. The content had to be concise and consistent.

Evaluating internal content is essential to determine whether it supports business strategies. Communications audits reveal opportunities to strengthen engagement and create more compelling material.

Years ago, when I launched my communications company, I advised clients to build their own "newsrooms" within their platforms. As social media grew and earned media became harder to secure, organizations had to take control of their own storytelling. Depending solely on traditional media was no longer viable.

When you start to look at the organization as a whole and every platform where messages are communicated, it becomes more of an audit, which should examine websites, social media, newsletters, blogs, podcasts, white papers, and speeches. Ask: What are we telling our audiences, and how are we reaching them? Writers and creators must research, collaborate, and understand the leader's voice as well as the organization's identity.

Designating a dedicated team of content creators elevates brand presence. These professionals ensure that every platform reflects the company's values, vision, and culture.

Messaging + Content = Alignment + Identity

Messaging inspires alignment internally. Content amplifies identity externally. Together, they ensure the organization speaks with one voice—clear, consistent, and compelling. As poet George Herbert said, "Good words are worth much, and cost little."

Step Into Messaging and Content Creation

"Good content isn't about good storytelling. It's about telling a true story well." – Ann Handley

Leadership Tips: Crafting Clear, Culture-Shaping Messaging
Theme: Leading Through Language That Resonates and Rebuilds

1. Start With Purpose
- Anchor every message to a clear "why"—inform, inspire, align, correct, or celebrate.
- Match tone to intent; a corrective message wrapped in celebration confuses.

Prompt: Before writing or speaking, ask: "What do I want them to understand, feel, and do?"

2. Simplify Without Losing Meaning

- Remove jargon and insider shorthand.
- Use accessible language without stripping nuance.

Prompt: Read aloud. If it wouldn't land with a new hire or frontline teammate, refine it.

3. Make Messaging Repeatable

- Consistency breeds clarity—craft phrases, metaphors, or stories others can carry forward.
- Train leaders to use the same framing to avoid dilution.

Prompt: What phrase or idea should echo in every team meeting?

4. Embed Cultural Narratives

- Messages should reinforce values, not just share information.
- Use storytelling, spotlight real people, and metaphors that reflect organizational identity.

Prompt: What cultural thread does this message strengthen—trust, growth, grace, or excellence?

5. Steward the Voice of Leadership

- The executive voice is more than strategic—it's stewardship, truth, and clarity.

Prompt: How can I better steward compassion and clarity through my words?

Messaging Blueprint: Lighthouse Edition
Metaphor: The Lighthouse

- **Foundation (Intent):** Know your "why" before you speak.

- **Beam (Clarity):** Shine truth in a focused, repeatable way.
- **Rotation (Reach):** Ensure words reach every part of the organization without distortion.
- **Structure (Values):** Build communication on trust, grace, and courage.

Reflection Prompts:
- What am I trying to communicate or shift?
- What phrase should be echoed across every team?
- Would this message make sense across departments?
- What value does it reinforce—grace, growth, honesty?

Leadership Tips: Improving Communication Content
Theme: From Polished to Purposeful—Sharpening Content That Connects

1. Refocus on Intent
- Clarify desired impact: inform, shift mindset, reinforce culture, or catalyze action.
- Filter content through strategic priorities and emotional resonance.

Prompt: What should your audience think, feel, and do after engaging with this?

2. Make Complexity Accessible
- Break down jargon with visuals, analogies, and structured summaries.
- Use storytelling to make abstract concepts tangible.

Prompt: What metaphor or image could help this concept "click"?

3. Humanize the Tone
- Move from transactional to relational—even policy updates can carry warmth.
- Audit language for clarity, compassion, and authenticity.

Prompt: Does this reflect how you'd speak face-to-face with someone you respect?

4. Invite Feedback Early
- Share drafts with trusted voices.
- Use iterative messaging—release, learn, refine.

Prompt: Who outside your circle could sharpen this content with honest input?

5. Align With Culture and Values
- Messages should reinforce organizational identity.
- Ensure storytelling echoes purpose and values.

Prompt: If someone read this without context, what would they learn about our culture?

6. Frame With Stewardship
- Speak truth with grace and intentionality.

Prompt: Am I building trust, clarity, and courage through my words?

Visual Framework: The Communication Lens
- **Metaphor:** The Lens
- **Magnifier:** Amplify key ideas or values.
- **Filter:** Remove jargon or excess noise.

- **Focus Ring:** Center on clear intent.
- **Frame:** Align with tone and culture.

Workshop Flow:
1. **Magnify Meaning:** Highlight core purpose—clarity, connection, challenge, or celebration.
2. **Filter With Compassion:** Revise for truth and grace.
3. **Focus for Impact:** Make next steps and values visible.
4. **Frame for Culture:** Ensure tone mirrors organizational DNA.

Stewardship Overlay:
Ask: Where am I being invited to sharpen clarity and soften tone—to speak not just as a leader, but as a light?

"Gossip hardens the heart and muddies the mind."
– Vanessa Denha Garmo

Insight 6: Water Cooler Conversations

From the latest TV drama to the most recent office party, the water cooler has always been the place where conversations naturally flow. Whether it's the water cooler, the coffee pot, the kitchen, or the breakroom, people gather throughout the day to connect, share stories, and build relationships—often in spontaneous, unplanned moments. Sometimes it is idle kibitzing.

My friend Mary Martin is a profound instructor and facilitator in faith formation. She is intentional about connecting with colleagues on a personal level, often asking about their family lives. While working at the Archdiocese of Detroit, she made it a priority to learn about the children and families of those she worked with. These heartfelt conversations not only strengthened professional relationships but also blossomed into enduring friendships.

Often sparked by casual water-cooler chats or chance encounters in the hallway, these moments of connection have left a lasting impact.

A study referenced by the National Institutes of Health (NIH) found that 49% of remote workers missed seeing their colleagues, and 14% specifically missed water cooler chats. The message is consistent and compelling: These casual, everyday interactions play a significant role in supporting employee well-being.

What if you know there is a chaotic culture at your company, but you are not aware of the conflicts or disconnects? Communications audits or assessments reveal gaps in your current internal and external communications. By inventorying all communication touchpoints, you can identify areas that need improvement or additional resources. Once you begin talking to employees, you start to see the holes, confusion, and other issues with how people communicate.

There is value in impromptu conversations with coworkers, such as when simply walking down the hallway. These casual conversations, commonly referred to as water cooler chats or water cooler conversations, involve informal discussions that colleagues engage in during breaks at work. While this form of communication can be lost with more employees working remotely, it's a chance for people to socialize and talk about non-work-related topics, such as hobbies and personal interests.

Some of my most valuable conversations at work happened in the in-between moments—walking the halls to refill my coffee mug or heading to the restroom. I'd bump into colleagues, and what started as casual small talk often unfolded into meaningful, insightful exchanges.

These conversations can help build company culture, improve collaboration, and promote employee engagement. So, the next time you find yourself chatting by the water cooler, know that it's not just a break—it's an essential part of fostering positive workplace relationships.

Although there is research that supports the benefits of water cooler conversations, they also should be monitored to prevent division among employees. Water cooler chats could lead to office gossip, and there is no value in gossip. I learned many years ago that gossip hardens the heart and muddies the mind, and it changes the company culture—not in a good way.

From a relationship perspective, gossip can be hurtful and damaging, leading to bruised feelings and reputations. It can also erode trust between colleagues and chip away at morale, leaving people feeling unsupported and uncomfortable in their work environment.

In addition, spending time on side conversations can decrease productivity at work. Managers and leaders need to monitor gossip to prevent time from being wasted and trust from being diminished.

Gossiping can also take a toll on employee health by increasing anxiety, especially when rumors circulate without clear information as to what is and isn't factual. When we retell painful stories of being hurt or wronged by someone, adrenaline spikes, and so does cortisol, which is a stress hormone.

Gossip can create a hostile work environment, which can lead to attrition as good employees leave the company. If you don't tell your company's story internally, someone else will tell your story and most likely get it wrong. If you want to reduce and even eliminate company gossip, be clear and consistent with your messaging. The prior chapters led to this point.

Water cooler conversations may seem small, but they're a powerful thread in the fabric of workplace culture. These casual touchpoints create connection in ways formal meetings simply can't. Here are some notable value points related to water cooler conversations:

Strengthening Relationships and Building Trust

When colleagues pause to chat about life, family, or the latest show they're watching, they're doing more than passing the time. They're building rapport. And when people feel connected, they collaborate with greater ease and empathy.

A Natural Release Valve for Stress

A light moment, a shared laugh, or a quick exchange about something unrelated to work can reset the tone of a stressful day. These small interactions help people breathe, regroup, and return to their tasks with a clearer mind.

Everyday Knowledge Sharing

Some of the best ideas surface in informal spaces. A quick conversation can spark a new perspective, offer a solution to a lingering challenge, or open the door to cross-department learning. These organic exchanges often fuel professional growth without anyone labeling it as such.

A Boost in Engagement and Belonging

When employees feel free to speak up, share their thoughts, and be themselves—even in casual moments— they feel more connected to the organization. These conversations remind people that their voice matters and that they're part of a community, not just a workflow.

Igniting Creativity and Innovation

Unstructured conversations invite curiosity. They give people room to think out loud, explore ideas, and build on each other's insights. Many innovative solutions begin not in a boardroom, but in a hallway conversation that sparks a new way of seeing a problem.

In the end, water cooler conversations are far more than a break from the day. They're a catalyst for connection, creativity, and a healthier workplace culture. When we honor these moments, we strengthen both the people and the organization—a true win.

An article from CoffeePals noted "25 common topics in watercooler talks," including office news; movies and TV; music; books; online trends; technology; weekend plans; celebrities; gratitude; challenges; family; pets; world events; vacations; hobbies and interests; holidays; food; politics; health; random advice; trivia; childhood memories; then-vs.-now comparisons, and the weather.

These topics can be great starters of conversation and an easy way to begin building genuine relationships with coworkers. We all need a core group of allies in the workplace—people we can trust, rely on, and lean into as we navigate our own strengths and weaknesses.

Step into the Water Cooler Conversations

"If more of us valued food and cheer and song above hoarded gold, it would be a merrier world." – J. R. R. Tolkien

Listening Beneath the Surface: Leadership Tips on Water Cooler Insights

1. Lean into the Informal

- **Pay attention to tone shifts:** Listen during casual cross-functional meetings, team lunches, or Slack threads. Humor, sarcasm, or silence can reveal subtle unrest or disconnection.
- **Walk the floor, not just the boardroom:** Drop into everyday conversations. You don't need to eavesdrop—just be present in spaces where real talk happens.

Prompt:

Where are people most relaxed and candid? What's the energy like in those moments?

2. Discern the Roots, Not Just the Rumors

- **Separate signal from noise:** Gossip often grows where there's a vacuum of clarity, consistency, or safety.
- **Ask reflective questions:** "What do you think sparked that?" or "What are folks concerned about?"

Prompt:

Is this conversation a symptom of missing information, misplaced trust, or genuine curiosity?

3. Empower Cultural Interpreters

- **Connect with trusted culture carriers**—those informal influencers who hear what's real and interpret it wisely.
- **Invite feedback, not surveillance:** Ask them what patterns they're noticing—not to report individuals, but to reveal cultural trends.

Prompt:

Who helps translate between leadership and the frontline with honesty and grace?

4. Repair What's Behind the Chatter

- **Don't "fix" gossip—heal the system:** Look for what's being misunderstood, misaligned, or miscommunicated.
- **Follow up with clarity:** Share truths gently and publicly when misinformation is spreading, but always protect dignity over dominance.

Prompt:

What's the truth that needs better storytelling? Is silence allowing confusion to thrive?

5. Framing: Wisdom over Reaction

Don't fear the comments being made; shepherd them with clarity, compassion, and grace.

Prompt:

Journal: *Where am I being called to bring light—not just correction—to informal conversations? How might gossip be transformed into growth with my presence and posture?*

Culture Champion Card

Theme: Tuning the Understory—Turning Gossip into Growth

The quiet talk in the margins often speaks loudest about what people believe, trust, and fear.

1. What Am I Hearing Between the Lines?

Consider:

- What's being said casually or jokingly that may hint at confusion, frustration, or fear?
- What questions or stories keep resurfacing?

Prompt:

Recall a conversation that lingered in your mind. What might it reveal about clarity, trust, or unmet needs?

2. Am I Amplifying or Anchoring?

Consider:

- When I hear gossip, do I add energy to it, or gently shift the tone toward understanding?
- What response reinforces dignity rather than drama?

Prompt:

Reflect on a moment when you helped redirect a reactive or gossipy conversation. What did you learn about your influence?

3. How Might I Tune the Cultural Current?

Consider:

- Could a story, celebration, or act of clarity help reshape the narrative?
- What simple truth needs more airtime?

Prompt:

What message—clarifying, encouraging, or faith-filled— could you share this week to ripple across informal spaces?

4. Framing: Quiet Influence with Sacred Weight

Even unplanned words carry spiritual weight. Tuning culture begins with whispers, not headlines.

Journal: *Where am I called to sow peace, truth, or encouragement in behind-the-scenes conversations? What posture reflects care over reaction?*

Theme: Culture Shifts in the Margins—Reading, Redirecting, and Redeeming Informal Chatter

Metaphors That Anchor the Message

- **Small messages make big waves:** A casual comment can shift team dynamics.
- **Attuned leaders resonate with clarity:** The right presences can recalibrate gossip.
- **Subtle conversations nourish culture:** Unseen talk may carry roots of real issues.

Areas of Focus

Location of Chatter: Where do informal conversations thrive?

Be present in relaxed, relational spaces.

Tone of Conversation: What emotional energy carries through gossip?

Listen to subtext, not just content.

Cultural Signal: What story is being told beneath the surface?

Redirect with clarity and compassion.

Redemptive Opportunity: Can this be used to clarify values or correct myths?

Frame truth gently, reinforce trust.

Leadership isn't just about strategy—it's about posture. Informal conversations reveal what's held in trust, pain, or misunderstanding. Our response can either mirror peace or magnify confusion.

Prompt:

Where am I being invited to be a presence of peace in the margins? What narrative am I called to redeem through presence, listening, or wise redirection?

"The kinds of errors that cause plane crashes are invariably errors of teamwork and communication."
– Malcolm Gladwell

Insight 7: Evaluating Effectiveness and ROI

I had a longtime colleague call me, frustrated by a lack of response. "How often do people ghost others?" he asked. "Is this common in the workplace today? Do you see this in your coaching sessions? I email people, but I get no response."

There's no universal rule for prompt replies. I follow my own 24-hour standard, though it differs from the familiar "wait 24 hours before responding when upset" guideline. A communications assessment helps organizations analyze strategies and tactics, revealing what works, what doesn't, and even how often people return messages.

Ghosting is more than an annoyance—it can be damaging to business. Ignoring a colleague is bad enough, but ignoring a customer is far worse. One of my clients enforces a four-hour rule: Customer inquiries must be answered within four hours. For coworkers, the standard is 24 hours unless the deadline is pressing.

That same colleague was also left hanging by an insurance agent from a major company. The agent had reached out to him about updating his life insurance policy, but after several attempts to follow up, he discovered the agent had been out of the office for days, with no indication on his voicemail that he was unavailable. Something as simple as updating an outgoing message doesn't cost a dime, yet failing to do it can cost you revenue when a client feels ignored. And if this small communication breakdown is happening, imagine the other disconnects that might be occurring across your organization.

It's imperative to establish response-time standards. Understanding current practices provides strategic insight, guiding decisions and opening opportunities for sustainable communication success. Epiphany Assessments/Audits build both strategic thinking and communication management skills.

Coaches often use question-guided conversations to spark reflection and insight. These open-ended questions lead clients to "epiphany" moments and promote critical thinking. Similarly, communications audits are intentional and purposeful, designed to uncover how people are sending and receiving information. They serve as a springboard for strategic planning.

As a consultant, I help clients use assessment/audit results to create actionable communication plans. Leaders can then measure the return on investment (ROI) of their efforts. Did communication improve? Did turnover decrease? Is gossip and confusion fading? These are the markers of progress.

Plans should be evaluated consistently. Quarterly reviews or check-ins during leadership meetings can track ROI and ensure the company is communicating effectively with employees, customers, and stakeholders. Success can be measured in many ways: increased business, stronger sales, new customers, or improved morale.

A communications audit isn't just about identifying problems; it's about creating clarity, building trust, and ensuring every message strengthens the culture and advances the mission.

By evaluating the effectiveness of communications tools and strategies, leaders can measure the ROI of their communications efforts. Once an assessment is completed, the leadership team can evaluate the results and create a strategic plan that can be executed to improve communications. They can then invest in resources and strategies.

On a consistent basis, they can evaluate the process and determine if the ROI was worth it and whether communication improved. Is there less employee turnover? Is communication more effective? Are there fewer company gossip incidents, less confusion, and defused chaos?

Communications plans can be evaluated throughout the year. Perhaps implement a check-in during regular leadership meetings to track the ROI of the strategic plan. This is especially important to ensure your company is properly communicating its message to its customers and stakeholders.

You can assess whether business has increased, your products are selling more, and you have gained new customers (depending on the business). Also, check to see if departments are more productive and if there is less confusion in the workplace. There are various ways to assess the ROI of a communications assessment.

"Management is efficiency in climbing the ladder of success; leadership determines whether the ladder is leaning against the right wall." – Stephen Covey

Evaluating Communication Effectiveness in the Workplace

Theme: Moving from Transmission to Transformation

1. Measure More Than Metrics

- Go beyond open rates and attendance logs—look for meaning, not just measurement.
- Use engagement indicators: Are conversations sparked? Are decisions clearer? Is morale rising?

Prompt: What outcomes—not just outputs—are directly impacted by our communications?

2. Listen Through Layers

- Create feedback loops across departments, levels, and cultures.
- Use surveys, shadowing, or listening sessions to uncover how messages are interpreted, not just received.

Prompt: Where might translation be needed—not across languages, but across lived experiences?

3. Assess Cognitive and Emotional Impact

- Clarity is cognitive. Resonance is emotional. Effectiveness requires both.

Prompt: Ask teams: "What's clear in our messaging?" and "What feels meaningful to you?"

4. Check Consistency Across Channels

- Review how the same message appears in email, meetings, handbooks, onboarding, or threads.
- Mixed signals confuse; aligned signals clarify.

Prompt: What story are we telling—through our words, tone, and timing?

5. Look for Storytelling That Sticks

- Effective communication becomes shared language.
- Listen for recurring phrases, metaphors, or reframes that signal internalization.

Prompt: What language is echoing back from teams? Is it aligned with our mission?

6. Stewardship of Truth and Tone

- Messaging reflects calling, clarity, and compassion.

Prompt: Are my words building trust, hope, and understanding—or just filling airspace?

Communication Effectiveness Diagnostic

Theme: Turning Words into Culture—Evaluating Clarity and Impact

1. Is My Message Clear in Head and Heart?

- Does it make cognitive sense and achieve emotional resonance?
- Do people leave more focused or foggier?

Prompt: What did people understand mentally, and what did they feel emotionally?

2. Are My Communications Creating Movement?

- Did the message lead to a decision, action, or dialogue?

Prompt: What ripple emerged—alignment, action, or silence?

3. Is My Message Consistent Across Channels?

- Did email, meetings, dashboards, and verbal remarks align?

Prompt: Did any platform create friction or confusion?

4. Is My Message Echoed Back?

- Are others repeating key phrases, stories, or values?

Prompt: What part of your communication shows up in others' words or behaviors?

5. Stewardship of Impact

- Your voice isn't just informative—it's formative.

Prompt: Where am I called to steward clarity with humility and courage?

Communication Effectiveness Visual Framework

Metaphor: Mirror and Signal

- **Mirror:** Reflects intent, tone, and integrity.
- **Signal:** Shows clarity, reach, and resonance.
- **Bridge:** Connects across roles and departments.
- **Echo:** Reveals repetition of values and language.

Exercise:

1. **Hold the Mirror:** Rate clarity, tone, and intent. Does this reflect values or contradict them?
2. **Tune the Signal:** Map how the message travels. Is it distorted, ignored, or amplified?
3. **Test the Echo:** Ask leaders or team members to paraphrase. What's remembered—and what's missed?

Measuring ROI on a Communications Audit

Theme: From Metrics to Meaning—Evaluating Strategic Impact and Cultural Return

1. Clarify What You're Measuring First

- Define success before launching: clarity, engagement, consistency, efficiency, and cultural alignment.

Prompt: What friction points do we hope to resolve—and what outcomes would signal success?

2. Track Strategic Alignment Gains

- Audit findings often reveal misalignment between messaging and goals.

Prompt: What decisions or campaigns could be reimagined once messaging matches mission?

3. Map Efficiency Improvements

- Disjointed communication costs time and trust.

Prompt: Where could clearer communication save time, reduce turnover, or prevent conflict?

4. Evaluate Culture and Engagement Impact

- Look for subtle wins: stronger participation, authentic feedback, deeper alignment.

Prompt: Are people more confident in voicing concerns and echoing the mission?

5. Use Audit Findings as Story Fuel

- Refined messaging strengthens branding, onboarding, and cohesion.

Prompt: What fresh stories emerged that can reinforce culture internally and externally?

ROI Visual Framework

Theme: Signal Strength and Trust Currency

- **Signal Strength:** Clarity, reach, and reliability of messaging → efficiency and reduced miscommunication.
- **Currency of Trust:** Value earned through consistent communication → retention, and engagement, reputation.
- **Leadership Lens:** Clarity of decision-making and cultural alignment → smarter strategy and measurable traction.

Stewardship Overlay: Communication as Calling

Communication effectiveness and ROI are not just strategy—they are stewardship. Every word shapes culture, trust, and legacy. Leaders are called to amplify truth with tenderness, clarity with courage, and culture with care.

Reflection Prompts:

- Where am I being invited to steward words with greater clarity and vision?
- How can improved communication multiply trust, grace, and momentum across this organization?

- What fruit has grown from my words—clarity, healing, unity—and what seeds remain unplanted?

Stewardship Thread: Your leadership voice is not merely functional—it is formational. Messages that echo truth, love, and direction leave a legacy far beyond their moment.

"Goals are pure fantasy unless you have a specific plan to achieve them." – Stephen Covey

Insight 8: Organizational Goals

One of my favorite practices—both personally and professionally—is working with goal sheets. Every year, I sit down to write out my goals, breaking them into categories and mapping out the steps that will bring them to life. It's a simple exercise, but it has the power to transform vague dreams into clear direction.

I'll never forget one of my earliest coaching clients. When I asked her to name just one goal for her life, she looked at me and said, "I don't get people who say, 'In five years I want to be doing this or living there.' I've never thought about my future, where I want to be, or where I'm going. I'm just living day by day." She was stuck in a rut—working a dead-end job, struggling to pay her bills, and unable to see the value of setting goals. Her story reminded me of a truth I share often: If you don't know where you're going, you'll never know how to get there.

This principle applies not only to individuals but also to organizations. Leaders must set goals, but more importantly, they must communicate those goals clearly. I once conducted a communications audit for a company where not a single employee could confidently articulate the organization's mission or goals. Each person gave me a different version of the vision statement and values. Without clarity, the team was adrift, and progress was impossible.

In coaching, clarity is everything. Clients don't just define their goals—they create strategies to achieve them. That means writing goals down, breaking them into manageable steps, and scheduling consistent time to work on them. One client, for example, was tasked with updating company process documents. Together, we used a CliftonStrengths-based model to design a plan. She committed to just 15 minutes a day, five days a week, documenting her daily tasks. Over time, those small, consistent efforts produced a valuable training resource for her team.

I once interviewed a handful of employees at a company, and not one of them could answer the question: what is the company's vision or goals?

Audits often reveal a common disconnect: Employees don't know the goals of the organization or the expectations of their managers. That's why I encourage leaders and clients alike to create yearly, quarterly, and monthly goals using structured goal sheets. Goal setting is not just about productivity—it's about vision, empowerment, and direction. It's about turning "someday" into "today."
So, I ask: How can you get anywhere if you don't know where you're going? If you're ready to start charting your path, you can request a goal sheet from my website at www.epiphanycommunications.com.

Step into Goal Setting

"A goal without a plan is just a wish."
— Antoine de Saint-Exupéry

Leadership Tips: Aligning Vision, Voice, and Strategy

Theme: Leading from the Core—Making Goals Visible and Actionable

1. Revisit and Rearticulate the Core Goals
- Goals must be more than words in a strategy deck— they should be visible, memorable, and story-rich.
- Reframe objectives with metaphors, values, and examples that resonate across roles.

Prompt: How often do team members hear and see our goals woven into daily communication, not just in formal documents?

2. Audit Decisions Against Goals
- Review policies, recognition systems, and resource allocations.
- Ask whether these reinforce the organization's stated goals or unintentionally create drift.

Prompt: Do my decisions quietly communicate something different than our mission?

3. Ground-Level Goal Interpretation
- Invite frontline and mid-level leaders to describe what goals mean in their roles.
- Look for disconnects or overly abstract language that needs grounding in practical action.

Prompt: How would a new team member define success based on our day-to-day behavior?

4. Evaluate Goal Messaging Streams

- Ensure branding, leadership updates, onboarding, and internal campaigns consistently reinforce strategic goals.
- Inconsistency between messages and actions breeds mistrust.

Prompt: Is our storytelling reinforcing our goals—or unintentionally fragmenting them?

5. Make Goal Alignment a Dialogue

- Use feedback tools, listening circles, and co-created narratives to keep goals alive.
- Create space for questions like, "Where do you feel connected—or disconnected—from our strategic direction?"

Prompt: What stories do people share about our goals—and do they match the reality we're building?

6. Faithful Stewardship of Goals

- Stewardship means embodying goals, not just naming them.

Reflection Prompt: In journaling or prayer, ask: *Where am I called to bring deeper clarity between what we say, what we do, and what God is asking of us? Which organizational goal needs renewed attention, storytelling, or alignment today?*

Alignment Reflection Card
Theme: Living the Mission, Not Just Naming It

Are My Decisions Echoing Our Goals?

- Do daily choices reinforce long-term objectives—or distract from them?

Prompt: Reflect on a recent decision. How clearly did it advance our stated goals?

Do My Messages Reflect Strategic Priorities?

- Are updates, announcements, and recognition tied to key outcomes?

Prompt: Scan your last few communications. How clearly do they connect to your mission?

Do Others Understand Our Goals Through Me?

- Can team members articulate what we're trying to accomplish because I've clarified it often and consistently?

Prompt: Ask someone outside your circle: "What do you think our main priorities are right now?" Does their answer reflect your influence?

Stewardship Prompt: In prayer or journaling, reflect: *Where am I invited to bring the vision into clearer view—through words, decisions, and example? What truth needs to be made plain so others can run with purpose?*

Visual Framework: Compass and Thread Edition
Theme: Weaving Goals into Culture with Direction and Intent

Leadership Workshop Flow

1. Center on the Compass
- Begin with the organizational North Star (mission, vision, strategic priorities).

Prompt: Where are we heading, and what needs recalibration?

2. Trace the Thread
- Map where communication, decisions, and recognition reinforce goals.

Prompt: What is being reinforced—not just announced?

3. Evaluate the Blueprint
- Analyze whether workflows, onboarding, or messaging platforms reflect goal alignment.

Prompt: Are we building with intentional coherence or reacting ad hoc?

Guidebook Series: Leading from the Core—Aligning Goals, Voice, and Culture

Modules Overview:
- **Communication Lens:** Sharpening clarity and intent.
- **Lighthouse Messaging:** Crafting memorable, mission-aligned messages.
- **Culture Tuning Fork:** Reading informal signals to understand alignment.
- **Compass and Thread:** Evaluating decisions against core goals.
- **Mirror and Signal:** Tracking clarity, reach, and resonance.

Activities and Exercises:

- Visual journaling pages with goal-focused prompts.
- Walkthrough cards for each metaphor.
- Dialogue labs for leader-led discussions.
- Story mapping worksheets to trace organizational narratives: What are we saying—and are we living it?
- S.M.A.R.T. Goal Sheets: Specific, Measurable, Achievable, Relevant, and Time-bound.
- Strengths-based Goal Plans

"The quality of a leader is reflected in the standards they set for themselves."
– Ray Kroc

Insight 9: Gaps and Opportunities

One of my favorite exercises to facilitate in group and team coaching is deceptively simple. I show the team a single picture—sometimes a busy street scene, sometimes a quiet landscape—and ask everyone the same set of questions: What do you see? What's happening? What's the problem? What's the solution?

Without fail, the answers vary dramatically. One person focuses on the people, another on the environment, another on the mood. Some see opportunity; others see risk. Some jump straight to solutions; others want more information. They are tied to their natural talents and their weaknesses. That is why self-awareness is essential in building strong teams and communicating effectively.

This exercise always sparks a moment of realization: We can look at the same situation and interpret it in completely different ways. And if that's true for a picture, imagine how differently we interpret emails, directives, expectations, tone, and feedback in the workplace.

A communications assessment functions the same way. It gives leaders a clearer view of the landscape they're working in. It uncovers the gaps, blind spots, and opportunities that often go unnoticed because everyone assumes they're "on the same page." In reality, most teams are not.

The Story of the Team That Thought They Were Communicating Well

A few years ago, I worked with a leadership team that believed their communication was strong. They held weekly meetings, sent regular emails, and had an open-door policy. But when I conducted a communications assessment, a very different picture emerged.

One employee said, "I never know what the priorities are. They change depending on who I talk to."

Another said, "I get emails at 10 p.m. and feel like I have to respond immediately."

A third said, "We hear about decisions after they've already been made."

The leaders were shocked. They weren't trying to create confusion—but confusion was happening anyway. The assessment revealed that each leader communicated differently, and employees were left trying to interpret mixed messages.

Once the leaders saw the gaps, they could finally address them. They created a unified communications plan, clarified expectations, and aligned their messaging. Within months, morale improved, turnover dropped, and productivity increased. This is the power of a communications assessment: It reveals the truth leaders need to lead well.

Why Communication Gaps Matter More Than Leaders Realize

Research consistently shows that communication breakdowns are one of the top reasons organizations lose productivity, engagement, and even revenue. Studies from Gallup have found that poor communication contributes to:

- Lower employee morale
- Higher turnover
- Increased conflict
- Missed deadlines
- Customer dissatisfaction
- Reduced trust in leadership

In other words, communication isn't a "soft skill." It's a business strategy. And when communication falters, culture falters.

A communications audit helps leaders identify where those breakdowns occur. It can reveal underserved employee groups, inconsistent messaging, unclear expectations, or channels that simply aren't working. What we say—and how we say it — shapes the culture more than any mission statement ever could.

The Story of the Silent Department

In one organization I worked with, the communications assessment revealed that an entire department felt invisible. They weren't included in key emails. They weren't invited to cross-department meetings. They weren't asked for input on decisions that directly affected their work.

When I asked the leadership team why, they were stunned. "We thought they preferred to work independently," one leader said. "We didn't realize they felt shut out."

The truth was simple: No one had ever asked.

Once the gap was identified, the leaders made immediate changes. They added the department to communication lists, invited them to planning sessions, and created a feedback loop. Within weeks, the department's engagement scores improved, and collaboration across the organization strengthened.

This is what happens when leaders stop assuming and start assessing.

The Hidden Disconnects That Sabotage Success

Leaders often assume they know what's being communicated across their organization. But unless they're intentionally assessing it, they're relying on assumptions rather than evidence.

A communications assessment helps leaders answer critical questions:

- What messages are being delivered?
- Who is delivering them?
- Are they consistent?
- Are they understood?
- Are they reaching the right people?
- Are they aligned with the organization's values and goals?

Gaps are created when different people deliver different messages, when expectations shift without explanation, or when employees feel left out of the loop. Confusion becomes the norm, and confusion is costly.

Another common gap is inconsistency in accountability. When one employee is corrected for a mistake while another is not, communication becomes unpredictable. People stop trusting the process—and eventually, they stop trusting leadership.

The Story of the Double Standard

During one assessment, employees repeatedly mentioned that one team member was allowed to miss deadlines without consequence, while others were reprimanded for the same behavior.

When I brought this to the leadership team, they were surprised. "We didn't realize we were treating him differently," one manager admitted. "He's been here so long, we just assumed he knew what he was doing."

But the team saw it differently. They saw favoritism. They saw inconsistency. They saw a gap.

Once the leaders became aware, they corrected the issue, clarified expectations, and communicated standards more consistently. Trust began to rebuild—but only because the assessment brought the issue to light.

Leadership Standards Must Be Lived, Not Announced

Whatever standards you set for your team, you must also model. Employees watch leaders closely. They notice when leaders communicate clearly—and when they don't. They notice when leaders hold themselves accountable—and when they don't.

This isn't about issuing orders from the top. It's about leading with your strengths, demonstrating emotional intelligence, and creating an environment where communication is honest, respectful, and consistent.

Gaps widen when leaders criticize people down instead of coaching them up. A communications assessment helps leaders see where their approach may unintentionally discourage, confuse, or silence their teams.

Turning Gaps into Growth Opportunities

The beauty of a communications audit is that it doesn't just reveal problems—it highlights opportunities. It shows leaders where they can elevate their teams, strengthen relationships, and build a culture rooted in clarity and trust.

When leaders partner with a leadership development coach, they learn how to:

- Communicate with intention
- Deliver consistent messaging
- Strengthen accountability
- Build psychological safety
- Coach rather than correct
- Align communication with organizational values
- Close the gaps that hinder performance

A communications assessment becomes a roadmap. It shows leaders where they are, where they want to go, and what conversations must happen to get there.

The Bottom Line

Communication is the heartbeat of culture. When it's strong, the organization thrives. When it's weak, everything else suffers. A communications assessment gives leaders the insight they need to identify gaps, leverage strengths, and create a culture where people feel informed, valued, and empowered.

The goal isn't perfection—it's awareness. Because once leaders see the gaps, they can finally begin to close them.

"A pessimist sees the difficulty in every opportunity; an optimist sees the opportunity in every difficulty."
– Winston Churchill

Leadership Tips: Gaining Insight into Gaps and Opportunities in a Communications Audit

Theme: Listening Beyond Words—Diagnosing Culture through Clarity

1. Scan for Strategic Silences

- Look for **what's NOT being said**—especially in change messaging, recognition, or internal branding.
- Gaps often appear where complexity is avoided, emotions are unaddressed, or values go unnamed.

Prompt:

What topics feel consistently not communicated across departments or leadership levels?

2. Assess Message Consistency Across Channels

- Compare tone, language, and purpose across formats (email, Slack, onboarding decks, all-hands talks).
- Inconsistencies may confuse teams or fragment cultural understanding.

Prompt:

Is the story of our goals and culture coherent, no matter where someone hears it?

3. Map the Messaging Journey by Role or Level

- Evaluate how different groups receive and interpret key communications.
- A message may land well at the executive table, but misfire on the factory floor or in hybrid environments.

Prompt:

Where might interpretation drift or information bottlenecks create blind spots?

4. Spot Missed Feedback Loops

- Gaps in two-way communication reveal opportunities for trust building.
- Explore whether people have clear channels to ask questions, share concerns, or reflect meaning.

Prompt:

Where might silence signal fear, fatigue, or disengagement—not agreement?

5. Uncover Opportunities for Culture Storytelling

- Look for spaces where values, wins, and personal stories could be highlighted, but aren't.
- Micro-moments (like shout-outs, onboarding anecdotes, or meeting reflections) build coherence and identity.

Prompt:

What story could be told more often—to reinforce what we value most?

Stewardship Reflection Prompt:

Where have I been silent when clarity was needed? Where is God inviting me to speak more intentionally—with courage, grace, and strategic hope?

Gap and Opportunity Reflection Card

Theme: Tuning the Narrative—Healing Friction and Amplifying Flow

Every gap is a grace-filled invitation. Every overlooked opportunity is a chance to restore alignment.

Stewardship Layer: Restoring Truth Where It's Been Missed

Gaps and silence in communication are prompts. They invite us to bring grace where there's fragmentation, and clarity where confusion has crept in.

Stewardship Reflection Prompt:

Where might you be nudged to name truth more clearly or speak healing into cultural blind spots? What opportunity is quietly calling for your leadership voice to rise—gently, bravely, and with love?

"Teamwork begins by building trust. And the only way to do that is to overcome our need for invulnerability."
– Patrick Lencioni

Insight 10: The Bully and the Bottom Line

When my friend and LinkedIn connection shared a July 2025 news story about a murder at a local McDonald's that was widely covered by the media in Michigan, I immediately wondered how this tragedy could have been avoided.

When communication fails, tragedy follows. As a coach, that was my reflection on the story.

The heartbreaking incident at the Eastpointe, Mich., McDonald's—where a young employee allegedly took the life of her manager following a public social media rant—left many stunned. But beneath the horror lies a sobering truth: Communication breakdowns in the workplace can escalate into devastating consequences when left unaddressed.

As a leadership coach, I don't just see a violent act—I see missed opportunities for intervention, empathy, and clarity.

What went wrong?

I don't know firsthand, since I wasn't there, but from what I read, a team member felt unheard, disrespected, and dismissed. A manager may have lacked the tools to de-escalate tension or recognize emotional distress.

The workplace culture failed to provide a safe space for feedback, conflict resolution, or psychological safety. During an Instagram rant, the employee repeatedly called the manager a bully. When feedback becomes gossip, and correction feels like punishment, trust erodes. When leaders don't know how to listen beneath the surface, pain festers.

This tragedy reminds us that:

- Leadership isn't just about authority—it's about emotional intelligence.
- Communication isn't just about words—it's about presence, tone, and timing.
- Conflict isn't the enemy—silence can be.
- Coaching can help leaders and teams build the skills to navigate hard conversations, recognize warning signs, and foster cultures of respect and resilience.

Let this be a wake-up call—not just for fast-food chains, but for every workplace. We must do better. We must listen better. We must lead better.

As I mentioned earlier, the high turnover of employees is a red flag that there is something wrong with the culture. Communications audits help identify when the problems stem from bullies in the workplace. I wrote my master's thesis on this topic, and in my research, I discovered that workplace bullies negatively impact the bottom line.

You may be able to stop a bully from bullying you, and I do share tactics with clients, but you can't stop a bully from being a bully unless that person wants to change.

What often happens is that the talented employees leave. The company or organization loses some of its most valuable staff members. Bullying can be discovered in a communications audit, and these are not isolated incidents. Bullying is consistent; it's not a one-off "mean behavior" issue. There are various tactics bullies use to overpower people, and they create toxic work environments.

Hopefully, you, as the leader, are not the workplace bully. It is a learned behavior, and if you bully, your staff will learn to do the same. Now you have created a very unfriendly environment that will not only repel talented people but also hinder growth and success.

Step into the Bottom Line

"Silence is Expensive: How Workplace Bullying Drains Your Bottom Line." – Nasdaq 2024

Theme: Confronting Toxicity to Protect Trust, Talent, and Trajectory

1. Recognize That Results Can Mask Harm

- Some high performers create bottom-line wins but leave a trail of emotional damage, fear, or disengagement.
- Long-term costs of bullying include turnover, absenteeism, legal risk, and brand erosion.

Prompt:

Is this person winning at the expense of others' well-being or trust?

2. Audit Communication Norms for Subtle Bullying

- Bullying isn't always loud—it shows up in sarcasm, exclusion, passive aggression, or manipulative behaviors.

- Review meeting behavior, email tone, Slack interactions, and public callouts.

Prompt:

What unspoken tones or patterns might be creating fear, confusion, or humiliation?

3. Assess Leadership Signals and Accountability

- Does executive silence enable toxicity from top talent or legacy leaders?
- Are performance reviews reinforcing behavior that undermines culture?

Prompt:

What message do we send when someone's results protect their mistreatment?

4. Listen to the Whisper Network

- Bullying often shows up in informal conversations, quiet exits, and stories shared in confidence.
- Create safe channels for upward feedback— anonymous if necessary—and act visibly on it.

Prompt:

What are people saying when they feel safe—and what are we doing with that truth?

5. Calculate the True Cost of Toxicity

- Losses include damaged morale, missed innovation, flight of great talent, and broken trust.
- Conduct exit interview audits, wellness surveys, and HR-complaint trend reviews.

Prompt:

What's the emotional and financial cost of keeping someone who erodes culture?

Stewardship Framing: Power with Accountability

Bullying is a misuse of power. As stewards of culture, leaders are called to confront wrongdoing with clarity and compassion.

Faith Reflection Prompt:

Where am I being called to protect the vulnerable—not just the visible? What leadership shift must happen to restore dignity and justice at every level?

The Bully and the Bottom Line

Theme: Seeing the Damage Beneath the Applause

Performance without integrity isn't success. It's erosion.

Stewardship Framing: Courage That Restores

True leadership confronts wrongdoing, not to punish, but to protect. When the bully is revealed, culture can begin to breathe again.

Culture Courage Series Framework

Theme: Protecting People, Purpose, and the Pulse of the Organization

Sample Retreat Activities:

- **Torchlight Walkthroughs:** Story-based case studies for evaluating moral courage
- **Culture Crack Mapping:** Team exercise to identify where trust fractures have gone unnoticed
- **Mask or Mirror Circle:** Leader reflection on image vs. integrity
- **Restoration Rituals:** Designing a response to harm through language, gesture, and structure
- **Stewardship-Fueled Forums:** Leadership-led dialogue on justice, leadership, and redemption

"You can't build a reputation on what you are going to do." – Henry Ford

Insight 11: Executing and Evaluating a Communications Plan

Just as financial or performance audits are essential to organizational health, communications audits should be conducted regularly. They provide valuable insights that strengthen messaging strategies and contribute to long-term success.

From Assessment to Action

A communications assessment begins with gathering information—through interviews, surveys, and observation—and culminates in a strategic plan. How an organization communicates directly shapes its culture, whether productive or toxic. This truth applies not only to workplaces but to families, communities, and any group that relies on shared understanding.

One effective tool is the S.W.O.T. analysis:

- **Strengths:** What is working well in communication?
- **Weaknesses:** Where are the gaps or inconsistencies?
- **Opportunities:** What new channels or practices could improve engagement?

- **Threats:** What risks—internal or external—could undermine clarity?

By listing and revising each area, leaders can refine the plan to address both immediate needs and long-term goals.

Turning Insights Into Strategy

After interviewing employees, the results are drafted into a report for management or HR. From those insights, a communications plan is created and presented to the organization as a policy—a roadmap for how to communicate consistently and effectively. These conversations don't just inform; they actively shape culture.

Plans should be executed over a defined period with regular check-ins. Leaders must track progress, note successes, and measure return on investment. Ask: What is improving, and what is not?

Case in Point

I once worked with a client determined to build a culture of success and motivation. After conducting an audit, we created and executed a communications plan. Within months, communication improved, and water cooler gossip nearly disappeared. By reorganizing employee charts and placing people in roles better suited to their strengths, we saw immediate, positive change.

Communication assessments aren't a one-and-done exercise. They should be woven into an organization's ongoing plans and policies, revisited regularly, and refined as teams evolve. When leaders treat communication as a living, continuous practice—not a single event—they build cultures that stay aligned, responsive, and healthy over time.

Measuring Results

Execution is only half the work. A system must be in place to assess improvements and answer the critical question: Is the culture improving?
Options include:
- Conducting a follow-up communications audit.
- Surveying staff for feedback on morale and productivity.
- Reviewing quarterly progress through culture and communications evaluations.

The Listening Tour

One of the most effective evaluation tools is a listening tour. Leaders can schedule one-on-one meetings, host town halls, or engage in impromptu conversations. By truly listening, leaders gain insights into the company's trajectory and uncover opportunities for growth.

The listening tour is more than a check-in—it's a practice of stewardship. It allows leaders to hear the heartbeat of the organization and ensure that communication is not only strategic but also human, authentic, and aligned with values.

Step into Execution and Evaluation

"If you don't tell your story, someone else will."

"What's your story?"

Theme: Measuring Impact That Moves Minds and Mission

1. Define Results Beyond Delivery
- Don't settle for "message sent"—look for message received, understood, and acted upon.
- Pair quantitative data (views, clicks, responses) with qualitative feedback (reactions, decisions, behaviors).

Prompt: Did this communication create clarity, momentum, or culture reinforcement—or was it just noise?

2. Evaluate Across Cognitive, Emotional, and Cultural Layers
- **Cognitive:** Was the information understood?
- **Emotional:** Did it generate confidence or concern?
- **Cultural:** Did it align with values and identity?

Prompt: What changed in how people think, feel, and behave after this message?

3. Assess Message Echo and Behavior Ripple
- Are key phrases, metaphors, or values being repeated?
- Did the communication shape follow-up conversations, decisions, or rituals?

Prompt: Where is this message showing up again—in language, action, or leadership tone?

4. Check Strategic Goal Alignment
- Did the communication move the needle on a specific priority?
- Review performance metrics, engagement scores, or alignment surveys.

Prompt: What measurable outcome did this message support—and how clearly?

5. Track Gap Closures and New Opportunities
- Did the message resolve confusion, realign a team, or open new dialogue?
- Use feedback loops to refine or reinforce.

Prompt: What problem did this message address—and what opportunity did it unlock?

Tools and Templates:
- **Rhythm Mapper:** Weekly, monthly, and seasonal messaging cycles.
- **Cascade Kits:** Talking points, visuals, and metaphors for manager briefings.
- **Feedback Pulse Tracker:** Reflection forms and listening touchpoints.
- **Story Echo Cards:** Prompts for leaders to reinforce messages with lived examples.
- **Message Impact Scorecard:** Track reach, clarity, resonance, behavior, culture echo, and strategic alignment.
- **Visual Echo Map:** Evaluate how messages ripple across direct echoes, behavioral shifts, cultural tone, and values.

Stewardship Overlay: Communication as Ministry

Executing and evaluating a communications plan is more than strategy—it is stewardship. Every message shapes understanding, belonging, and trust. Leaders are called to amplify truth with tenderness, clarity with courage, and culture with care.

Reflection Prompts:
- How can my words reflect both truth and grace?
- Where am I being invited to amplify values, not just transmit information?
- What fruit has grown from this message—clarity, healing, unity?
- What seeds remain unplanted, waiting for my voice to nurture?

Stewardship Thread: Your leadership voice is not just functional—it is formational. Each message carries the power to guide, heal, and unite. Communication becomes legacy when it is rooted in love, clarity, and courage.

Summary

Background Information

A communications audit/assessment entails a comprehensive review of your organization's communications and uses feedback from your stakeholders to determine what's working, what isn't working, and where improvements can be made.

What is the Purpose of a Communications Audit?

A communications audit determines the effectiveness of your current communication tools, highlights their strengths and weaknesses, and provides suggestions and recommendations on how to improve them. It serves as a systematic research method for identifying the strengths and weaknesses of your current internal and external communications.

Through the audit, we can determine:

- What are you communicating?
- How are you communicating?
- Are your communications effective?

An effective communications audit will identify:

- How past communications were handled
- Target audiences: what they currently know about the company/organization, services, products, etc.; what they need and want to know; and how they prefer to be reached
- Strengths and weaknesses in current communications programs
- Untapped opportunities for future communications

Plus, a well-executed audit has the potential to:

- Understand employees' channels for updates, whether email, intranet, team meetings, or other platforms. *Are there too many distractions created by CCing all employees?*
- Gauge the effectiveness of communication from immediate supervisors. *Are managers proactive in sharing relevant information?*
- Explore how team collaboration impacts communication. *Are colleagues supportive and communicative?*
- Assess employees' awareness of organizational objectives. *Do they understand the bigger picture?*
- Probe employees' emotional connection to the company's future. *Are they invested in its success?*

Internal – We Can Assess:
Communications across the board within the entire organization, including:
- Emails
- In-person meetings
- Phone meetings
- Texting
- Team meetings
- Supervisor to supervisor
- Department to department

Who we interview:
- Leadership
- Department heads
- Supervisors
- Teams
- All or selected employees

Conduct S.W.O.T: Strengths, Weaknesses, Opportunities, and Threats

Research Method Options
To conduct your assessment/audit, we can use different research methods:
- One-on-one interviews (Via Zoom or phone)
- Focus groups (by department via Zoom)
- Email questions

Think Like a Communications Consultant and a Coach!
Based on our findings, what would we recommend for future communications? We can select team members to help us analyze the audit results and strategize future actions.

Fundamentally, this should provide the company with a much-needed cultural change around how we communicate. We must educate folks that communication is a product, and the product is data. Everyone must understand how to quickly identify the criticality of communication and know when to pick up the phone, when to text, when to team chat, or when to email.

If you have a high turnover of employees, it just might be the company culture. There are articles and studies examining why people leave. They reveal that, in many cases, people leave silently, but as a result of a toxic culture. Exit interviews are valuable conversations to better understand why employees leave. Never underestimate the power of effective communication to create a productive culture!

Once the audit is complete and assessed, coaching is a natural next step; it's a significant way to close the gaps.

Cultivating Leadership After Listening: The Value of Coaching Post-Audit

After conducting a communications assessment, organizations often discover pockets of misalignment, silos of misunderstanding, or untapped strengths waiting to be amplified. Leadership development and team-building coaching are the next faithful steps toward restoration, clarity, and empowered connection.

Why Coaching After an Assessment Matters

- **Bridges Between Insight and Action:** Coaching ensures that the audit doesn't just reveal gaps—it equips leaders and teams to close them thoughtfully and courageously.
- **Tailored Growth for Each Layer of Leadership:** For emerging leaders to seasoned executives, coaching allows personalized reflection and development around key findings, fostering agility and emotional intelligence.
- **Rebuild Trust in the Message and the Messenger:** When communication has faltered, coaching offers a safe, guided space to reestablish credibility, transparency, and a consistent voice.

Team Building That Resonates

- **Renews Shared Purpose:** Team-building exercises, especially those anchored in organizational values and mission, help teams reconnect to the "why" behind their work.
- **Fosters Psychological Safety:** Coaching helps surface what's unsaid or unclear with team building, then creates the relational conditions for honest, restorative dialogue.
- **Strengthens Collaborative Capacity:** Insights from the audit become opportunities for role clarity, cross-functional trust, and healthier feedback loops.

Stewardship-Infused Impact

- **Provides a Chance for Renewal:** Audits sometimes uncover disconnects—coaching can invite spiritual reflection, forgiveness, and recommitment to service.
- **Clarifies Ethical Leadership:** Coaching provides space to examine integrity gaps and align leadership behaviors with stated values.
- **Encourages Stewardship of Influence:** Leaders are reminded that their words shape culture. Coaching helps them carry that responsibility with humility and vision.

Bridge and Compass Framework

A Post-Assessment Guide for Leadership Renewal and Team Reconnection

1. The Bridge: From Awareness to Action

This represents the intentional journey from communications audit findings to restored trust and leadership clarity.

- **Anchors:** Audit insights, stakeholder feedback, and moments of truth
- **Supports:** Coaching conversations, reflection tools, and ethical case studies
- **Pathway:** Aligned messaging, empowered leadership behaviors, and shared purpose

"Leadership is the bridge that carries culture, trust, and truth forward" - Stephen Covey

Once the bridge is built, the compass keeps leaders oriented—especially when tension, change, or complexity arises.

- **North:** Organizational mission and spiritual vision
- **East/West:** Individual strengths, team dynamics, and cross-functional collaboration
- **South:** Ethical grounding, humility, and accountability

Values are the True North of influence. Without direction, communication becomes noise.

Applications and Reflections:

- Facilitate **workshops** to help teams align their internal messaging with their collective goals.
- Translate into **reflection cards** or a visual handout for coaching sessions.

- Adapt for a **stewardship-rooted keynote or column:** exploring how restoration begins with leadership listening and continues through intentional redirection.

Resources

Office of Behavioral and Social Sciences Research. *"The Future of Work: Evidence-Based Considerations for Hybrid and Remote Work."* National Institutes of Health, 10 Jan. 2023, https://obssr.od.nih.gov/news-and-events/news/director-voice/future-work-evidence-based-considerations-hybrid-and-remote.

CoffeePals Team. *"25 Things Often Talked About in Watercooler Conversations."* CoffeePals, 12 March, 2025. https://www.coffeepals.com/blog/25-things-often-talked-about-in-water-cooler-conversations

"What Eastpointe McDonald's Worker Said in Instagram Rant 2 Days Before Allegedly Killing Manager; Afeni Muhammad Being Held on $25M Bond." WDIV Local 4, 11 July 2025, *https://www.clickondetroit.com/news/local/2025/07/11/what-eastpointe-mcdonalds-worker-said-in-instagram-rant-2-days-before-allegedly-killing-manager/*

Chamine, Shirzad. *Positive Intelligence: Why Only 20% of Teams and Individuals Achieve Their True Potential and How You Can Achieve Yours. Greenleaf Book Group Press, 2012.*

Gallup. "CliftonStrengths." Gallup, (gallup.com in Bing)

About Vanessa Denha Garmo

Vanessa Denha Garmo is a certified life and leadership coach and a certified CliftonStrengths® Coach. She works with numerous clients on leadership and career development, communications, and team building. She has created the Epiphany Communications Assessment for individuals.

Her programs and resources focus heavily on a growth mindset and developing emotional and positive intelligence. She uses a brain science approach to coaching when helping clients get unstuck, which often centers around mindsets and beliefs. She helps people and organizations reach their goals, lead with strengths, and build strong teams.

She also enables clients to create a leadership style focused on communications and strengths, empowering them to unleash the leader in themselves and awaken the spirit of success.

Vanessa is the founder of Epiphany Communications: Coaching and Consulting. She and her team serve as communications evangelists, strategists, consultants, and content writers. They conduct a communications assessment to comprehensively understand an organization's communications practices, strategies, and channels. Through coaching, Vanessa's clients have Epiphany moments where they grow deeper self-awareness.

Vanessa has more than 25 years of experience in communications. She is the host of *Epiphany* on Ave Maria Radio and was a full-time reporter for WJR 760 AM in Detroit for 10 years. She hosted the radio program, *It's Your Community*, which was heard on WJR, 96.3 FM, and 93.1 FM for 30 years. As an award-winning journalist, Vanessa guides clients on how to tell their stories using various platforms. And, as a speaker, facilitator, and consultant, she tells her audiences: "Everyone has a story to tell, but if you don't know *how* to tell your story, no one will care about your story."

Vanessa co-founded the *Chaldean News* and served as co-publisher and editor-in-chief for nearly 16 years. She has a bachelor's degree in journalism and a master's in communications, and she wrote her thesis on bullies in the workplace. She is also an Emmy® Award-winning documentarian. You can follow Epiphany Communications on Facebook and Vanessa Denha Garmo on X, Instagram, TikTok, and LinkedIn. For more information about Epiphany, visit www.epiphanycommunications.com

Want to learn more about a communications assessments? Schedule a complimentary inquiry call by reaching out to Vanessa at www.epiphanycommunications.com; via email at info@epiphanycommunications.com; or by phone at (248) 830-8605.

About Professional Development

I help organizations build stronger leaders by teaching managers how to use their strengths to create high-performing teams.

I do this by delivering strengths-based leadership workshops that help new managers and team members lead with greater confidence. I also offer one-on-one coaching. If your team is planning development programs, I'd be happy to share a few tailored options.

As a certified Life, Leadership, and Strengths Coach, I specialize in leadership development, strengths-based coaching, and communication training. I also offer the Epiphany Communications Assessment that measures your personal communication style. My work helps emerging leaders understand their natural talents, improve how they show up, and build teams that are more aligned, resilient, and effective.

I blend CliftonStrengths, Positive Intelligence (PQ) training, communications assessments, and practical leadership tools with real-world strategies so leaders can lead with clarity, confidence, and purpose.

I also facilitate "Power Hour Professional Development Sessions" for organizations that can be tailored to their needs. These sessions are 60 minutes and focus on areas of

Strengths and Weaknesses, Identity, Communications, Leadership, Team Building, Positive Intelligence, and Growth Mindset. I can also tailor a 12-month training program that focuses on leadership development and creative, productive work cultures.

Example Programs:

- "Strengths-Based Leadership for High-Performing Teams" (2-part series workshop or half-day workshop)
- "Leadership Development and Team-Building Training" (12-month program)
- From Assessment to Action: Learning from the Way People Communicate (90-minute session)
- "Team Reboot: Rebuilding Trust and Collaboration" (Tailored)
- "The Creation Code: Understanding and Applying Personal Transformation through a Growth Mindset" (15-part series)

Coaching:

- One-on-one coaching
- Group coaching
- Leadership development
- Strengths-based coaching (CliftonStrengths)
- Communication and team alignment
- New manager training
- Culture and engagement
- Conflict resolution
- Executive coaching
- Career Coaching
- Onboarding Strategies
- Goal Setting

What Clients Are Saying ... In Their Own Words

"Vanessa Denha Garmo has been an invaluable partner to MIRA during one of the most important transitions in our organization's history. As a seasoned leadership development coach and communications consultant, she guided our board with wisdom, clarity, and collaboration in identifying and preparing the successor for our new president and CEO. Vanessa's expertise in fostering strong communication and building alignment among diverse stakeholders ensured that the process was not only thorough but also deeply respectful of our mission and culture. Her ability to blend strategic insight with a collaborative spirit made her an indispensable resource, and we are grateful for her role in helping us move confidently into the future."

– Bobby Hesano, chairman of the Midwest Independent Retailers Association and President/CEO of D&B Grocers, Wholesale and Distributors

"As the former chairwoman of United Community Family Services, I saw firsthand how critical it is to select a leader capable of advancing our mission. When it came time to identify and hire a new president and CEO, Vanessa Denha Garmo's guidance proved invaluable. Her keen ability to evaluate leadership qualities, align individual strengths with organizational needs, and coach the candidate throughout the process gave us complete confidence in our decision. Vanessa's strategic approach ensured the candidate was not only an excellent fit but also well prepared to succeed in the role. Vanessa's contribution was instrumental to a smooth and successful leadership transition. Her expertise and dedication to leadership development have made a lasting impact on our organization."

– LeeAnn Kirma, former chairwoman of The United Community Family Services-Chaldean American Ladies of Charity

"I had the pleasure of working with Vanessa Denha Garmo over the last 12 years and have personally known her for 30 years (time flies). I can confidently say she is a remarkable professional. Vanessa has a unique ability to unleash leadership potential, helping individuals discover their strengths and develop their own leadership styles. Her expertise in creating and communicating effective messaging is truly impressive. Vanessa not only understands the nuances of communication but also knows how to tailor messages that resonate with diverse audiences and where and with whom to place these messages. Her guidance has been invaluable in helping me, and many others, grow professionally and personally. I highly recommend Vanessa to anyone looking for a seasoned professional who excels in leadership development and communications strategy."

– Christine Lints Longroy, Advanced Manufacturing Collaborator and Promoter

"When I was promoted to Chief Operating Officer at Blink Marketing Logistics, Vanessa's insights on communication and strategy in managing other people elevated my ability to coach and serve my team. Her approach of leveraging strengths and finding opportunities to connect with my employees improved my view of what it takes to be successful with several tiers of employees reporting to me. I also asked Vanessa to coach other key employees at Blink, and she led group sessions with our sales and management teams. I would recommend her for anyone searching for a mentor to challenge their leadership style for the better. I have many pages of notes that will last me throughout my career."

– Lee Dunn, CEO, Blink Marketing Logistics

"Vanessa is simply amazing. I have taken several of her courses over the past year and each one leaves you thinking about the strategic path you are on! I really enjoyed her perspective that she shared in her Networking class. It is the little things in life, whether it be business or personal, that will set you apart from your competition. Highly encourage anyone considering a coaching session(s) or taking a class with Vanessa to not hesitate."

– Jennifer Dickow, Automotive Purchasing Professional

"I trained with Vanessa for a little over a month in career transition, and I was able to enhance my skills in how to be more efficient when it comes to what my long-term desire was in a professional sense. Most importantly, she taught me that it is just as important to know what you don't want as what you want. The training was different because it was in a group setting, and that allowed everyone to hear different stories and experiences."

– Tiffany Habib, Senior Patient Recruitment Specialist, Headlands Research